Man
and Beast

Approaches to Anthropology

Today, the study of anthropology is at the heart of the humane sciences. From being an activity largely concerned with describing, tribe by tribe, exotic cultures, it now presents a multi-lensed set of spectacles through which to view all human behaviour.

In the last twenty years anthropologists have tended to draw from the ideas of others – historians, sociologists, psychologists, economists, zoologists, linguistic scholars and philosophers. Now the position is beginning to be reversed – and the hitherto particular interests of anthropology are being seen as of vital relevance to the understanding of the human animal in his individual, interpersonal and social manifestations.

Approaches to Anthropology, edited by Professor Mary Douglas, aims to illuminate the concerns of anthropologists to those in other disciplines and to a wider public. Each book will present an aspect of man's behaviour analysed through a number of approaches. The subject-matter and the method used to describe and analyse will be of equal importance. These original approaches will be exploratory, interpretative and demystifying and will help break down some of the artificial barriers between traditional disciplines, opening up a deeper understanding of the study of man.

Mary Douglas is Professor of Anthropology at University College, London, and the author, among other books, of two revolutionary works, *Purity and Danger* and *Natural Symbols*.

Roy Willis

Man
and Beast

Basic Books, Inc., Publishers
New York

Copyright © 1974 by Roy G. Willis
Library of Congress Catalog Card Number: 74–768 29
SBN: 465–04332–1
Printed in Great Britain
74 75 76 77 10 9 8 7 6 5 4 3 2 1

Contents

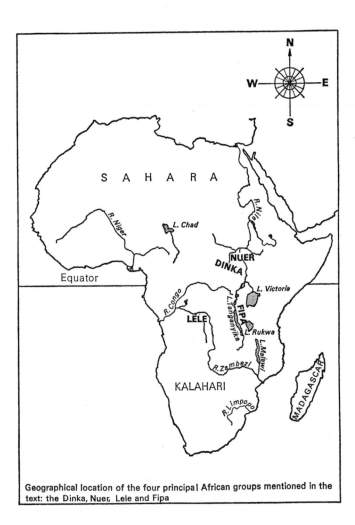

Geographical location of the four principal African groups mentioned in the text: the Dinka, Nuer, Lele and Fipa

Introduction

I am interested in what animals signify to man. I am also an anthropologist of a 'structuralist' persuasion, meaning that I find pleasure in discovering the way symbolic ideas are interrelated within human society and culture, and the (often recondite) connections of these ideational systems with social organization. In what follows I hope to have conveyed something of the interest and even excitement attending such investigations.

Let me explain how this book was written. It began with no more than an embryonic notion that the way men related to animals could, when subjected to the detailed examination of a structuralist analysis, be used as a key to 'read off' certain otherwise inaccessible information about the way human beings conceived of themselves and the ultimate meaning of their own lives. I then put this idea to the test of a comparative analysis of three discrete and dissimilar African societies. For the material on two of those societies, the Nuer and the Lele, I have drawn upon the rich and abundant evidence provided by E. E. Evans-Pritchard and Mary Douglas. The third society, the Fipa, I have studied at first-hand. Doing things this way led me to certain conclusions about the aims and methods of social anthropology which it is well to make explicit at the outset.

One surprising result was that I did not find any difference in principle between analysing societies at second-hand through the published work of two acknowledged masters of the subject, and analysing my own field material. In all three cases the work involved an exercise in imaginative reconstruction, based on the evidence, of what Husserl calls the 'life-world' (*Lebenswelt*) of each society. At this level, each social world so constructed has the same epistemological status: each was just as 'real', and valid in its own right, as the others.

Even so I do not think I could have undertaken such an exercise in the case of the two societies with which I am personally un-acquainted without having shared the experience of the ethnographers of the Nuer and the Lele of prolonged immersion in an exotic culture, so that reconstructing the worlds of the Nuer and the Lele was, no less than with the Fipa, a reliving of the ethnographer's self-translation into and out of an alien social universe. In Chapter 2 I indicate the successive stages of this process.

Guided by my major objective of deciphering the significance for Nuer, Lele and Fipa of the man–animal relation, I was able to deepen my analysis of each society by a series of structural comparisons. The Nuer sense of distance from, and equality with, the counterposed world of wild nature contrasted markedly with the Lele sense of the dependence and moral inferiority of the village in relation to the forest, and again with the Fipa sense of the village's properly dominant role in relation to the surrounding bush. These cultural differences in the perceived structure of the universe correlated with differences in ideas of time, of historical consciousness or the lack of it, and in ideas of the self. In this way, through a succession of imagined confrontations with different cosmological assumptions, each society and culture took on a more definite and specific form – as it were, affirming and strengthening its own identity in relation to the alien others. The end result was pictures of the Nuer, Lele and Fipa that differed somewhat from the published interpretations in the case of the first two, and especially from my own conceptions of the Fipa when beginning this book. Throughout it I try to show how significant new insights emerge in the course of cross-cultural comparison.

This was still not the final stage of the analysis, which addressed itself to the question of the meaning for each society of the man–animal relation. By this time it was possible to establish that in each society the relation consisted of a hierarchy of symbolically significant animals, with one animal at the apex of the hierarchical pyramid: the ox, in the case of the Nuer; the pangolin, for the Lele; and the python, for the Fipa.

I argue that these three beasts symbolize, for these three societies, the ultimate value – what we might call the 'meaning of life'. If my analysis is correct, what these animals symbolize is, respectively: transcendence of individual personality in pure, inner selfhood; transcendence of individual differentiation in pure communalism; and pure becoming, or developmental change, both social and personal. I try to show that these apparently speculative and highly abstract matters are in fact capable of precise formulation and logical demonstration.

The question that remains, of course, is why animals, as opposed, for instance, to inanimate objects of the earth or sky, should be the bearers of this supreme symbolic function. Why, as John Berger has noted, 'Animals supply examples for the mind as well as food for the body. They carry not only loads, but principles.'[1] Berger is commenting here on Francis Klingender's superbly documented study of European pre-Renaissance animal symbolism,[2] but the point is equally valid for our three contemporary African societies. The crux of the explanation of the apparent universality of animals as images of profoundest symbolic significance would seem, I argue, to lie in the fact that 'the animal' is both within us, as part of our enduring biological heritage as human beings, and also, by definition, outside and beyond human society. The image of the symbolic animal is therefore necessarily a dualistic image, structurally homologous with the duality in human society and the human self between the real and the ultimate ideal, the actual and the longed for, even if subconsciously.

Such is, summarily exposed, the formal argument of this book. But the book is also, and simultaneously, a reflection on the significance of social anthropology and of its characteristic method, especially as developed in Britain, of intensive and sustained field research. For in developing the analysis it was gradually forced upon me that in the relation of men to animals symbolic of transcendental values I was dealing not only with a secret cipher about ultimate human ideals but also with a metaphorical statement of what social anthropology is about, and by implication the meaning of the confrontation between 'the West' and the variegated 'other cultures' of the globe. Briefly my argument here is that the ultimate justification for social anthropology is not that it adds to the storehouse of objective 'facts' about undocumented or poorly documented societies, but its potential (as yet largely unexploited, I believe) for enlarging human self-knowledge. And the latter of course includes the self-knowledge of 'Western' people about themselves and their culture.

The two parallel strands of thought – the formal analysis of animal symbolism and the critique of social anthropology – come together in the closing chapters where the values of Nuer, Lele and Fipa are compared with Western ideals. The case of the Fipa in particular raises problems concerning the direction of social evolution where there is a dominant ethos of 'rationalization', such as characterizes both Western and Fipa society. But the outcome, it is suggested, is not necessarily a convergence towards an infinitely subdivided culture coordinated by an omnipresent bureaucracy, such as Weber prophesied. The meaning of the symbolic animals remains always, like the animal itself, in some measure beyond conscious and rational comprehension.

The treatment of animal symbolism in this book may suggest comparisons to some with the Jungian concept of archetypal images as products of a hypothesized collective unconscious. I do not wish to venture into these deep and, for me, intimidating waters, beyond suggesting that the kind of analysis developed here might be capable of providing a rational explanation for the provenance of such images. The rest I gladly leave to those competent to discuss the matter.

To readers acquainted with social anthropology the extent of my intellectual indebtedness will be apparent. Here I would particularly like to mention my lasting gratitude to Professor Sir Edward Evans-Pritchard, both for the inspiration of his thought and example and for his countless personal kindnesses to me; to Professor John Beattie for his stimulating and humane teaching and the enduring warmth of his friendship; and to Professor Mary Douglas for asking me to write this book and helping it into shape with numerous comments, both shrewd and sympathetic.

Edinburgh, 1972

1 Soulful Ox, Historic Wild Beast

The Nuer of the southern Sudan were for long something of a puzzle to ethnography. Evidently lacking any kind of formal government or judiciary, they nevertheless managed to preserve a measure of social cohesion and a sense of cultural identity among nearly a quarter of a million widely scattered people. When the basic principles of Nuer social organization were investigated in the mid-1930s by the British anthropologist E. E. Evans-Pritchard they turned out to be elaborations of a single idea, that of patrilineal descent. What this common anthropological term means is that in Nuer society the most basic social rights and duties, those concerned with the ownership of cattle, are, theoretically, transmittable through males only.* It may seem surprising that such a simple idea could coordinate the interests and activities of thousands of people dispersed over wide stretches of savannah. Here is how it works. Let us imagine that there was once a man called England. He had three sons, Northern, Midlands and Southern and they settled in three different regions of England's country, founding new communities there. Certain of their sons in turn left their paternal communities and founded new ones. The sons of Southern included Essex, Surrey, Hampshire and so on, while Northern's territory was divided between sons such as Cumberland, Northumberland and Durham. A further generation saw the founding of new and smaller communities within these territories. Colchester and Chelmsford, for example, left their father Essex and set up new communities, and from these in turn sprang new and smaller ones, and similarly in other parts of English tribal territory. Under this arrangement,

* Nuer occasionally 'fiddle the system' by transmitting such rights through women, but in such cases they preserve the integrity of the patrilineal principle by pretending to themselves that such women are really men. See also p. 64.

anyone in the country can eventually trace his descent back to the founding ancestor, England, but his primary allegiance will be to the branch of the colonizing family which is settled in his 'home' territory.

Nuer society is organized on these lines. The ideology of patrilineal descent and kinship, sometimes called *agnation*, validates territorial occupation. A common pattern of groups with sub-groups 'nesting' inside them runs through the whole tribe.*

With a single all-pervading pattern structuring their social relations, it is not surprising that Nuer conceive of the animals in their environment as organized in an analogous way. Evans-Pritchard says they speak of animals, as they do of themselves, in terms of *cieng*, or local community, and *thok dwiel*, descent group or lineage. There is, for instance, the community of the *jiciengngang*, the growling folk of tooth and claw such as the lion, the leopard, the hyena, the jackal, the wild dog and the domesticated dog. A lineage of this carnivorous community are the mongooses, which divide into a number of smaller lineages of little animals: the brindled mongooses, the white-tailed mongooses, the cerval cats, the civet cats, the genets and so on.[1]

The homology between the social world of the Nuer and their concept of the animal world is apparent. A simple mental operation has transformed the numerically small size of a recently founded, genealogically subordinate lineage into a subordinate lineage of physically small animals, in relation to the large carnivores.

Similarly, another collection of animals are spoken of as a community because they are normally found in or near rivers and marshes: the crocodiles, monitor lizards, all kinds of fish and marsh birds. Geese, duck and teal are a lineage within this riverine community of animals. Like the Nuer themselves, each individual animal is thought of as having his descent group allegiance and his spatial location by virtue of that allegiance.

The Nuer attitude to wild creatures seems to be that of a keen but detached observer: it is that of a scientist. As a rule he dis-

---

* There are several such 'tribes' in Nuerland, each forming a self-contained society organized according to the same principles. They thus resemble nation-states. Like nation-states with a common culture, Nuer tribes feel an affinity for each other and are capable of acting in concert against an external threat.

dains hunting, seeing wild animals 'as something in their own right, and his disposition is to live and let live'. Their world is a transformed mirror-image of the Nuer's own society. They are both different and alike, affording the possibility of a meaningful relationship of a metaphorical kind between the two worlds.*

It is quite a different matter with the pre-eminent domestic animals of the Nuer, their cattle. In contrast with the minimal interaction that Nuer have in reality with wild animals, there is the closest possible physical interdependence between Nuer and their herds. It is hardly possible to exaggerate the intimacy of the contact between the human and the bovine worlds. Evans-Pritchard has some passages on the subject:

> The men wake about dawn at camp in the midst of their cattle and sit contentedly watching them till milking is finished. They then either take them to pasture and spend the day watching them graze, driving them to water, composing songs about them, and bringing them back to camp, or they remain in the kraal to drink their milk, make tethering-cords and ornaments for them, water and in other ways care for their calves, clean their kraal, and dry their dung for fuel. Nuer wash their hands and faces in the urine of cattle, especially when cows urinate during milking, drink their milk and blood, and sleep on their hides by the side of their smouldering dung. They cover their bodies, dress their hair, and clean their teeth with the ashes of cattle dung, and eat their food with spoons made from their horns. When the cattle return in the evening they tether each beast to its peg with cords made from the skins of their dead companions and sit in the windscreens to contemplate them and to watch them being milked.[2]

Cattle are used to obtain wives, when they are paid as bride-wealth; possession of them is a frequent cause of dispute and violence, and when a man is killed as a result it is in cattle that compensation is made; and they are victims in ritual sacrifice. It is not therefore surprising that, as Evans-Pritchard says, 'Nuer tend to define all social processes and relationships in terms of cattle. Their social idiom is a bovine idiom.'[3]

Nuer conceive of cattle as socially identical with their own lineage system, as organized in herds which in their ties of descent and kinship duplicate the patrilineal relations of the descent groups owning them. Evans-Pritchard remarks that this idea is a fiction

---

* We shall see below that this possibility is realized as an expression of certain significant events.

because cattle are constantly being dispersed and replaced by others at marriages; but it is a true reflection of the fact that 'cattle are the core round which daily life is organized and the medium through which social and mystical relations are expressed'.[4] We can say that the ideas of social groups and cattle are interchangeable and equivalent in Nuer thought. They are not themselves in relation but are synonyms for one referent: a cattle-oriented, even cattle-obsessed, human society.

Nuer use their cattle to make metaphorical statements about both their own society and the natural environment, particularly the world of wild animals. They serve as a two-way bridge between the human and the natural spheres. Nuer cattle thus seem relevant to what the French anthropologist, Lévi-Strauss, has called 'the central problem of anthropology, viz., the passage from nature to culture'.[5] The same authority has developed a theory of what has been called 'totemism', according to which social groups are conceptually linked with natural species in many tribal societies not because the animals or plants concerned are good to eat, but because they are 'good to think', ready-to-hand counters in man's intellectual structuring of the universe. Nuer cattle are neither entirely utilitarian nor are they conceived abstractly as many peoples, including the Nuer, conceive of wild species. They permit themselves to eat their cattle only as a sequel to a ritual sacrifice.*

But the practical and mystical services do not exhaust the meaning of cattle for the Nuer. More than 'good to think', they are 'good to feel' and 'good to imagine'. Their function is aesthetic, not intellectual. This is because the Nuer is too much identified with his cattle to think about them in the abstract and detached way of the scientist, as he can with wild animals which touch his concrete existence only peripherally. But in talking of cattle he is pre-eminently an artist.

Evans-Pritchard outlines the complex of terms employed by the Nuer to describe cattle, giving us an idea of the wealth of imagery available to the Nuer in this idiom. According to Nuer usage, proper identification of a cow depends on its colours and the pattern in which they occur on its body.

---

* Nuer see the slaughter of cattle on these special occasions as one side of a reciprocal killing, because cattle are the indirect causes of many deaths.

'There are ten principal colour terms: white (*bor*), black (*car*), brown (*lual*), chestnut (*dol*), tawny (*yan*), mouse-grey (*lou*), bay (*thiang*), sandy-grey (*lith*), blue and strawberry roan (*yil*) and chocolate (*gwir*).'[6]

But this is only the basic vocabulary. Commonly two and sometimes more colours are combined in various patterns and Evans-Pritchard says there are several hundred named colour permutations. The names are often those of animals, birds, reptiles and fish, thus establishing an association between cattle and the natural environment. Thus the word *lou* means both a mouse-grey cow and a bustard, *nyang* (striped) is the crocodile, *dwai* (brown with white stripes) is the female sitatunga, *kwe* (white-faced) is the fish eagle, *kwac* (spotted) is the leopard, *cuor* (speckled) is the vulture, *gwong* (spotted) is the guinea-fowl and *nyal* (brown-spotted) is the python. Further elaborations of these metaphoric associations give the Nuer *rual mim*, charcoal-burning, or *won car*, dark clouds, to mean 'black ox'; *riem dol*, red blood, or *rir dol*, red tree-cobra, for 'red ox'; *bany yiel*, blue heron, for 'blue roan ox'; and *duk lou*, the shady gloom of forests, for 'mouse-grey ox'.

Further names specify the shape of the horns. There are at least six common designations in use, besides several 'fancy names'. They are combined with the colour and pattern terms to make many more possible permutations, while a further range of permutations is provided by the prefixes denoting the sex or age of an animal.

Cattle terms not only link them with the natural environment, they also merge cattle with their human owners through the custom of ox-names. Every Nuer takes one of his names from the term by which one of his oxen is described, and women also take names from oxen and from the cows they milk. This custom results in what Evans-Pritchard calls a 'linguistic identification' of men and oxen, so that a Nuer genealogy often sounds like an inventory of a kraal.[7] The double linguistic association of men with cattle and cattle with wild nature accounts for much of the metaphoric and poetic resources of Nuer imagery.

The Nuer, like most pastoral peoples, are poetic and most men and women compose songs which are sung at dances and concerts or are composed for the creator's own pleasure and chanted by him in lonely pastures and amid the cattle in camp kraals. Youths break into song, praising their kinsmen, sweethearts, and cattle, when they feel happy, wherever they may be.[8]

Evans-Pritchard gives an example of such a song, in which the poet ends by addressing his favourite ox as his 'friend':

> White ox good is my mother
> And we the people of my sister,
> The people of Nyariau Bul.
> As my black-rumped white ox,
> When I went to court the winsome lassie,
> I am not a man whom girls refuse.
> We court girls by stealth in the night,
> I and Kwejok
> Nyadeang.
> We brought the ox across the river,
> I and Kirjoak
> And the son of my mother's sister
> Buth Gutjaak.
> Friend, great ox of the spreading horns,
> Which ever bellows amid the herd,
> Ox of the son of Bul
> Maloa.[9]

There are several things to be noticed about this song. Firstly, it interweaves three major concerns of Nuer life, especially the life of the young men: cattle, sex and kinship. Secondly, there is much emphasis on matrilateral ties. This is a reflection of the fact that Nuer are very mobile. They go where they please. Often a man and several of his brothers will leave their natal village, taking with them what cattle they can appropriate, and set up with a married sister and her husband's people. This does not disrupt the patrilineally-based social organization, because the migrants simply transfer their loyalties to the dominant lineage in their new community.

Thirdly, the poet's ox is addressed as a 'friend'. Relationships of friendship are only just beginning to receive consideration in anthropology, but it would seem that the essential feature of friendship is a sense of likeness. Otherness is out, or at least in so far as it exists it is an obstacle to friendship, and is minimized by both parties. Yet friends also give to each other, and as soon as this giving stops the friendship ends sooner or later. But what is it that a friend gives, this other whose otherness is no part of the relationship and is therefore excluded from it? On the basis of the Nuer evidence I would suggest that a friend is basically valued as an interpreter of the world and a mediator between it and the self (this view implies that the common idea that friends are valued in their own right is a fiction). In the Nuer song the son of Bul Maloa praises his white ox as 'friend' with good reason. For it is through the bovine aesthetic that Nuer imaginatively relate to the cosmos. Cattle, as we have seen, bridge the worlds of society and nature, enabling both to be experienced in a common language.

This bovine language of the heart is no doubt a source of deep consolation and satisfaction to the Nuer, a people who live constantly at the margins of subsistence. But man is not only a feeler and imaginer, he is also an intellectualizer – a faculty which, in so far as primitive peoples are concerned, has received rather more than its due share of emphasis in the work of Lévi-Strauss. Nuer, like many other tribal peoples, select objects from their natural environment and set up conceptual relations between these objects and social groups. Most often, though not invariably, the objects so selected are animals.

We have already seen that the world of wild creatures stands juxtaposed to Nuer society as a transformed mirror-image. Here is the possibility of relationship between the human community and the different, yet proximate, realm of animals.

And such relationships are in fact set up from time to time. Any unusual event can originate an association of a 'totemistic' kind. Evans-Pritchard gives examples showing how such associations can begin and how, once established, the association may be retained in the consciousness of the people concerned.

'The story is told that long ago some people of *cieng* Gangi were dying of thirst on a journey. They were wandering, light-headed with thirst and the heat of the sun, when they saw a monitor lizard in a *thep*-tree (*acacia verugera*). They intended to kill it but it escaped them and following it brought them to water, to which, being a water creature, it naturally made. Ever since, their descendants have respected the lizard and dedicated cows of their herds to the lizard-spirit.'[10]

The miraculous escape of this group's ancestors is commemorated through a continuing association between group and reptile. (They also have a relation with the *thep*-tree for the same reason.)

A man on whose head a vulture once landed had a totemistic relation with vultures. If his descendants continue the observance the relation becomes a group one, otherwise it ceases with the man's death. The crucial factor is the social significance of the man – which in Nuer society means whether or not he is the founder of a lineage.

What is the function of such relationships between men and objects of the environment? Lévi-Strauss's interpretation of 'totemism', a category to which this kind of relation seems *prima facie* to belong, places the emphasis on the relations between the various discrete species, which then make up a relational system juxtaposed to, and understood as a metaphorical expression of, the corresponding system of human groups. Are we dealing with such a cognitive system in the case of Nuer 'totemism'? I think not. The system is not of the classificatory kind proposed by Lévi-Strauss, but is a method by which historical events, in an ahistorical society, are incorporated into the consciousness of those concerned with them. For the Nuer, the most common kind of such events is the founding of new lineages (or, what amounts to the same in the story of the monitor lizard, the miraculous salvation of an existing one).

To demonstrate this argument, several disparate strands of Nuer thought have to be considered. Evans-Pritchard emphasizes the abstract way in which Nuer conceive of totem relations. What are linked, in the case of a group totem, are two abstractions: the descent line and what Evans-Pritchard translates as the 'spirit' of the animal. Nuer are explicit about it. What they relate to in a totem relation is not the concrete animal but the immaterial essence or spirit (*kwoth*) of the species as a whole. To drive the distinction home still further, they often distinguish animal and 'spirit' by calling them by different names. *Nyal*, python, has a spirit called *fadiet* or *ulengdit*; lion (*lony*) has a spirit called *joo* or *cuar*; and so on. And the disjunction is further emphasized by saying that the various animal 'spirits' live in the sky, according to Nuer the abode of 'spirit' (*kwoth*) in the most abstract sense, while the material animals are on earth.

The formal shape of the relation is apparent. It involves a keeping of a distance between the two contraposed abstractions,

lineage and animal essence, the idea that in English is rendered
by the suffix '-ness'. (So that 'lion-ness' would be an appropriate
synonym for 'lion spirit', etc.) The quality of a distanced relationship is called *thek* by the Nuer, and translated by Evans-
Pritchard as 'to respect'. *Thek* is used not only of an individual's or
a group's relation to a totem, but of the attitude and behaviour
expected of a man towards his wife's parents and to a lesser extent
her other kinsmen. He expresses *thek* particularly by not eating in
their homes and not appearing naked before them.[11]

The most obvious breach of the proper respect, a failing to
observe the proper distance and coming into a forbidden close
contact is entailed when an animal representative of a totem
relation is killed, and *a fortiori* if the animal is also eaten. In such
a situation the sense of forbidden contact between animal essence
and human being is expressed in Nuer consciousness as a kind of
possession of the human by the animal spirit. It is as though the
animal essence, in that situation of unwonted contact, stamps its
mark on the human being concerned. Evans-Pritchard gives the
example of a man called Cam. Although not a member of the
Leng lineage, which had lion-spirit as its totem, he had close
ties with it through marriage and residence. Nevertheless he one
day killed a lion. Cam returned home 'bending his fingers like
claws and crouching as though he intended to spring on the
people around him. A sheep was at once sacrificed to the lion-
spirit, and Cam composed himself.'[12]

The relation and the requirement of *thek*, or distance, is held to
be reciprocal. Thus 'those who respect crocodiles enjoy a special
immunity from their attacks and I have been assured by old men
when about to wade through crocodile-infested streams that I
need have no fear, because people whose totem was the crocodile
lived nearby, and they contrasted the benevolence of their local
crocodiles with the savagery of crocodiles in other districts'.[13]

We are now ready to tackle a more complex idea in Nuer
thought about man–animal relations. This is the common
explanation given of a totemic affiliation that an ancestor was
born as twin to the animal concerned. This is a way of saying the
same thing in three different ways at once, repeating the same
message in three different codes to make certain it gets home.
Remembered ancestors are founders of descent lines, otherwise
they would not be remembered. To found a new line is to break

the social structure, to innovate: it is a historic event. And this even though, or rather because, the innovation is assimilated into the existing segmentary structure, so it is both the same and not the same after the event. A human twin-birth is conceptualized in the same pattern of split unity: twins have two physical bodies but they are one social person (*ran*), according to Nuer. Like a historical event, their birth is a sign of the intervention of *Kwoth* (spirit). Because of this, and to distinguish them from ordinary men, Nuer call human twins birds, because birds are the creatures closest to the primary abode of Spirit, which is the sky.*

When therefore Nuer explain a totem relation between social group and animal species by saying that an ancestor was born as twin to an animal they are asserting their social identity, expressed in terms of the reciprocal relation between group and species; they are remembering the historic event of lineage foundation, which is expressed in an image of human–animal twin-birth which is a 'mythical charter' for the totem relation. The association of animal and human is a sign of *Kwoth*, it is achieved through the agency of this unpredictable external force that Evans-Pritchard calls 'God' and 'Spirit'. Twinship is itself, as we have seen, a sign of the intervention of '*Kwoth*'.

What is the meaning of this complex of images? Professor James Littlejohn of Edinburgh University has suggested that twins are frequently 'chosen' as founders of lineages.[14] But I would think it is more likely to be the other way about: lineage-founders are invested *ex post facto* with honorary twinship, and moreover with the specially memorable kind of twinship that consists in being born twin to an animal.

In other words, when the Nuer say '*Kwoth*' in this context we can translate it as 'history'. For it is in terms of this kind of

---

* Nuer say that twins *are* birds, not that they are *like* birds. I here summarize an intricate argument by Evans-Pritchard on the meaning of this Nuer doctrine which has been the cause of much learned debate. See, in particular, Raymond Firth's 'Twins, Birds and Vegetables' (*Man*, N.S. 1, 1, 1966, 1–17) and G. B. Milner's 'Siamese Twins, Birds and the Double Helix' (*Man*, N.S. 4, 1, 1969, 5–23). Both these writers attempt to explain the Nuer twins–birds equation in terms of supposedly cross-cultural categories, such as 'taboo' and 'intuition', to my mind a perilous undertaking before the place of these and other symbolic concepts in the structure of Nuer cosmology has been properly understood. I return to this problem in Chapter 4 and in the concluding chapter. What I would hold on to for the moment is Evans-Pritchard's contention that the 'twins are birds' doctrine has to be comprehended in relation to a third term, the Nuer concept *Kwoth*.

man–animal image and relation that historic events are incorporated in the consciousness of the groups concerned and carried forward into the present. What at first glance appears to be a Lévi-Straussian synchronic classification is in fact a record of process, a segmented history. Here again, the further development of this argument in later chapters of this book will enable us to formulate this conclusion in more precise and sociologically significant language.*

The Nuer evidence as it has appeared thus far presents us with a picture of a society in which domesticated animals, primarily cattle, are used to initiate and maintain individual and social life in the most basic sense. The Nuer lives cheek-by-jowl with cattle from the earliest age, their bodies give him food, warmth and household utensils, their exchange makes possible marriage and settlement of disputes, and their sacrifice is essential to the propitiation of spiritual powers. But cattle are even more than this. They provide the Nuer with a wealth of poetic vocabulary which he uses to endow both his social life and the world of external nature with meaning. Human group and bovine herd are completely symbiotic. If the Nuer are parasites of the cow, as Evans-Pritchard observes, it could be said with equal justice that cattle are parasites of the Nuer, since this people devote the bulk of their lives to the welfare of their beasts. The latter are able to live their 'gentle, indolent, sluggish lives' thanks to the ceaseless ministrations of the Nuer. In return the cow mediates for man. She shields him from hunger and cold, enables him to initiate, maintain and restore social relations, and dies for him in ritual sacrifice. In this last situation indeed, according to Evans-Pritchard, there is total identification between animal and man, the beast dying as a surrogate for man, meeting a ransom demanded by God. Cattle mediate also the artistic needs of the Nuer, a people without writing or plastic arts, inspiring a metaphoric language capable of embracing the whole Nuer universe.

With the world of wild creatures the Nuer have quite a different sort of relation. Instead of being intimately involved with their own life and feelings, the world of wild nature is pictured as distant, though formally similar in structuration to the ramified divisions and subdivisions of Nuer social organization. He respects wild animals, finding hunting an unworthy occupation and

* See especially pp. 63–65.

the flesh of wild game an inappropriate fare for mature man. The model proposed to explain the distant relationship of mutual respect between human and wild animal society is that between collateral descent lines in Nuer society: what is called in Nuer a *buth* relationship. We have seen that organizational changes are commonly interpreted by Nuer as the intervention of *Kwoth*, 'Spirit' in the form of a wild animal, and that such 'events' are commemorated as distanced, *thek* relations between two abstract ideas: the 'spirit' of the animal concerned and the descent line; and that the event, and the relation, are often presented together in the compound image of an ancestor born twin to a wild animal.

Before pursuing further the dialectic of heart and head, soulful ox and intellectualized wild animal in Nuer culture, we need a basis for detailed comparison which will enable us to develop more widely relevant categories of man–animal relation. With this object we shall turn first to a people who in social organization and cultural emphases present some fundamental contrasts with the Nuer: the Lele of the Kasai province of the Zaire Republic.*

* Formerly the Republic of Congo (Kinshasa) and the Belgian Congo.

2 Paradox of the Pangolin

Just as the human foetus is said to recapitulate during its uterine life the various stages of man's evolutionary journey, so the anthropologist undergoing the field experience finds himself rehearsing the successive phases of his discipline's theoretical development. His first impulse on arriving in the strange community is to compare his hosts' way of life with his own: consciously or not, he evaluates it against an absolute standard, as would any robust Victorian. Then his interest necessarily turns to an inquiry into how the alien society works, how the different pieces of the institutional jigsaw fit together: he is now willy-nilly a straightforward functionalist of the 1920s. In due course he may find certain pervasive patterns in the thought and behaviour of his hosts infiltrating from his subconscious and assuming architectural form in his Western-analytic mind: he has become a structuralist, a man of the sixties. Finally, if he is unusually percipient and fortunate, he may succeed in transcending the past altogether and adding something to man's self-awareness.

This developmental process inside the anthropologist reflects the fact that anthropology, under whatever name, has been from the beginning an enterprise involving a critical approach not only to the primitive, but also to the metropolitan society. The Victorians made no bones about it (they hoped to deduce general laws governing *all* societies from their study of the 'rude races') and contemporary instances abound in the work of anthropology's present avant-garde. Only during the long Malinowskian interlude was it seriously maintained that 'tribal society' could be studied in the mode of a natural science, as a passive object; while simultaneously the functionalists' evocation of an idyllically harmonious 'Native' life expressed, albeit obliquely, their hatred of modern industrialism. There is no escape from relevance to his own society in the anthropologist's interpretation of the alien one. The more 'objective' he manages to be, the more clearly his results validate themselves as the outcome of a process of interaction between the disparate societies, a process mediated through the personality of the anthropologist himself, as a thinking and feeling being. (The price he pays for this privileged role is to be, in the end, fully a member of neither society, peripheral as a prophet or a spirit-medium.) In approaching the animal symbolism of the Lele, Bantu inhabitants of the fringes of the Congolese rain-forest, it may be illuminating to re-create in imagination the successive stages in which they, and their conditioning environment, took shape and assumed depth in the mind of their ethnographer, Mary Douglas.

The physical look and feel of the place are the first impressions recorded by this professional stranger, the anthropologist. In the Kasai province of Zaire, where the Lele people live, the forest is obtrusive and rather forbidding; only later does she learn that it is quite other for the Lele. The climate is generally unwelcome to a European: hot and dusty in the dry season, oppressively humid in the wet. The first sight of a settlement is inevitably memorable. Lele villages are surrounded by rectangular palisades; inside, rectangular huts are evenly spaced. Already there is the suggestion of an obsessive concern with boundaries and subdivisions.

Each settlement stands alone, situated in open savannah but never far from the forest's edge. Within the forest are streams from which the village women draw water. There are also cleared patches in which village families – a man and his wife, or wives, working together at complementary tasks – cultivate maize, manioc (cassava) and raffia palms. The grassland immediately surrounding the village is used by the women alone for the cultivation of groundnuts.

These isolated oblong settlements are the highest units of Lele social organization, analogous to sovereign states. If we compare Lele with a Nuer type of social organization, a comparison that Professor Douglas herself makes at the beginning of her published analysis (1963, 2), the equivalent would be the Nuer tribe, a scattered spread of localized settlements interrelated, as described earlier, like so many Chinese boxes, each nesting inside another up to the all-encompassing tribal 'box'. In contrast to this diffuse and open social universe, the Lele world is at once dense and isolated.

The anthropologist's inquiries into the workings of the Lele social system confirm the impression of careful balance and order suggested by the rectilineal precision of their building. Village residents are grouped according to their membership of an age-set system, all men of one age-set living adjacent to one another, regardless of clan affiliation. Unlike Nuerland, where the patrilineal descent system provides the basic idiom by which society is ordered, the Lele descent system, which is matrilineal, is essentially auxiliary to the main principle of organization, the system of village-based age-sets. Clans have no corporate existence.

In a typical Lele village the division of residents into older and younger sets is cross-cut by another division which allies the oldest set with the next but one below it in the age hierarchy, as against the set immediately below the most senior, which is itself allied with the youngest set. By this procedure, as Douglas observes, each of the two senior sets was allied with one of the two junior sets, resulting in 'a neat balancing of opposed interests in the village'. Members of allied age-sets not only lived close together within each village society, they also joined together in communal hunts, when 'the juniors had the benefit of the experience of the seniors of their own half, while giving the latter the advantage of their strength, speed and accuracy'.[1] There is a rigorous separation of the sexes which necessitates a close interdependence in the division of labour.[2]

The same principle of balance governed the allocation of the few specialized offices within each village society. The headmanship was a nominal post, held by the senior male member of one of the village's founding clans. The decisions he expressed were not his own, but the summation of a consensus reached by all the adult male residents. Another office-holder, the *itembangu*, had the dual duty of giving public expression to what could be seen as justifiable complaints made by one resident against another, and of keeping the village treasury. The *itembangu* was a member of one of the younger age-sets. Each age-set also had its own *itembangu*, entrusted with the task of regulating rights and obligations within it. None of these office-bearers, as Douglas emphasizes, wielded authority: 'In spite of their regard for

25

seniority, their political inclinations tended always towards balance, rather than to authority delegated from any peak to subordinate points in the system'.[3]

Yet this was also a society which rewarded disproportionately, in Douglas's estimation, precisely that section of the adult population which contributed least in terms of productive labour to the maintenance of the community: the old men. This was the group which in every village had the major share of women and wealth, the chief goods of Lele society. The question then occurred of how the unproductive, privileged elders retained their favoured position in the absence of any organized machinery of repression. Evidently their relatively fortunate state depended on the consent of the rest of the village. But how and why was this given?

Douglas discovered that the social status of every adult man was defined in terms of a complex of rights and obligations relating to wealth, particularly in the prestigious form of woven squares of raffia, and women. Rights over women were transferable. This was the institution of *bukolomo*, which Douglas translates as 'pawnship'. *Bukolomo* rights and obligations extended back into the past and forward into the future: men inherited them and gave and received promises of pawnship over unborn girls. Disposing of women meant wealth from their suitors, in the form of raffia squares; and there was the bonus that custom allotted a man's daughter's daughter to himself, to dispose of in marriage and so produce additional marriage payments. This system meant that men spent their younger life working to pay off acquired and inherited debts and saving to pay the substantial bridewealth, while in their later years they received payments and enjoyed polygyny. Debts were acquired easily: an insult, an ill-considered accusation of sorcery, was enough to make a man liable to claims for damages.

In theory Lele society was an equitable one. Over time it duly rewarded those who knew how to operate within its complex rules. This realization, Douglas suggests, was the basis of the consensus which upheld the privileges of the politically powerless older men. She also suggests more than this: that for the Lele wealth and women are not the ultimate end, that the complex game in which these goods are the counters had become for them an end in itself. '. . . the Lele did not even seem to think of the system as one which gave extrinsic advantages to the winners, or disadvantages to the losers. They always spoke as if sufficient explanation of the moves they made is contained within the rules of the system itself, as if it were a game played for its own sake.'[4]

The patterns of rights and obligations relating to pawns are so complex that it is impossible to abstract from them any clear idea of a final allocation of power, rather as in a modern capitalist society with its tangle of interlocking directorships. 'A man who was lord of clan x was likely himself to be a pawn of a man of clan y, while other members of y might be pawns of his own clan.'[5]

Here was a rule-governed society which had realized the utopian dream of peace and order without compulsion (within each village society, that is: between different villages, as between modern nation-states, war was endemic). But, as Professor Douglas discovered, albeit slowly, the Lele universe comprised another, dark world of symbolism which strangely mirrored the meticulous book-keeping of their secular life.

This hidden world, necessarily the last that comes to the knowledge of an anthropologist, is constructed out of the forest and its wild creatures. Lele men spend a great deal of time hunting and for them, unlike the Nuer, it is the most prestigious occupation possible. Nuer interest in wild animals is detached and impartial; Lele observe because it helps them in tracking and killing their prey. So many of the criteria by which they classify animals have to do with their behaviour: their sleeping, watering and feeding habits. These criteria, according to Douglas, 'give the Lele categories in which there is consistency among the secondary characteristics, so that different species* can be recognized. Carnivorous animals have fur and claws as distinct from vegetarian animals, such as the antelopes with their smooth hides and hoofs. Egg-laying creatures tend to fly with wings. Mammals are four-footed and walk or climb, and so on.'[6]

Evidently these are practical distinctions which a people who depend on wild flesh for food would naturally learn to make. The categories appear to rest on inductions from a number of observations in the best scientific–empirical manner. There is no

---

* Douglas would here seem to be referring to the more inclusive Linnaean category 'order' (e.g. the carnivora, the cervidae) rather than the subcategory 'species'. It would be interesting to know to what extent the Lele do distinguish zoological species (breeding populations) within these orders.

suggestion here of a meta-theory lying behind the simple taxonomy. The same cannot be assumed of another set of classifications which the Lele apply to the wild fauna of their environment. These distinctions are formally similar to the dualistic, cross-cutting divisions of Lele social organization. 'Animals of above' (*hutadiku*) are opposed to 'ground animals' (*hutahin*); day animals to night animals; and land to water animals.[7]

This second classificatory scheme, in contrast to the first, has no practical value to the Lele huntsman. It has to do not with the practical necessity for the hunter of differentiating between the various wild animals according to their appearance and behaviour, distinguishing between predator and prey, and so on, but with a basic cognitive need to integrate conceptually the world of wild nature, as a complex totality, in the wider universe of which human society is a part. This scheme groups animals in sets of paired opposites, just as men are grouped and opposed in the age-set system, both by reference to habitat: above/below, land/water; and in relation to the alternation of day and night, which is also a part of human experience. Strict rules apportioning social activities between daytime and night-time (e.g. women are not allowed to pound grain, a day activity, after dusk) are evidence of the significance Lele attach to this temporal dualism (ed. Forde, 1954, 12).

That for the Lele there existed an invisible, elaborately structured symbolic order which was largely populated by wild creatures was not, as we have seen, immediately apparent to their ethnographer. The existence and hidden dimensions of this dark world emerged gradually from a study of food taboos observed by Lele women. What they refused to eat, and sometimes even to touch, were animals which because of their appearance or behaviour resisted classification in the Lele scheme.

Food taboos remind us how potentially dangerous an activity eating is. It involves the assimilation into the body of external matter. Now the human body is itself, as Mary Douglas has made us aware, an elemental 'natural symbol' for society.[8] We therefore find in all cultures dietary prohibitions that ensure that what is ingested is always symbolically as well as nutritionally beneficial. The most intimate and private acts of human beings are fraught with social implications. Perhaps no people known to anthropology is more conscious of this essential dualism in human nature than the Lele, living as they do in a fine tension between inward and outward self, calculation and contingency, creativity and ritual.

Douglas lists a number of creatures which the Lele women refuse to eat. The tortoise is avoided because of its peculiar shell, and because it lays eggs like a bird but walks on the ground with four legs; the yellow baboon is prohibited because of certain oddities of behaviour, as Lele see it. Baboons are 'unlike other animals in that they will stand up to a man, they experience barrenness, they wash, and they undergo one of the ordeals of initiation' (they are said to shelter in deep gullies, such as diviners have to descend into during their initiation rites).[9] Pregnant women are held to be especially vulnerable to symbolically inappropriate food and have to avoid all water creatures which are associated with 'spirits'. All these prohibitions are backed by ritual sanctions. Douglas mentions only one avoidance which is not so sanctioned. Women refuse to have anything to do with the scaly tail, or 'flying squirrel', because 'they are not sure what it is, bird or animal'.[10]

It is not clear from Douglas's account why the 'flying squirrel' should not be the object of a ritually-backed prohibition like the others. Conceivably the explanation is that this creature differs from the other prohibited animals in that it is the only one not distinguished as anomalous by the symbolically significant classification which opposes 'animals of above' to 'ground animals'. Rituals are indicators of symbolic weight, alerting those who participate in them to the larger, potentially cosmic, significance of their acts. But we are still far from understanding the full meaning of the world of wild creatures in the Lele universe. Douglas insists on the cardinal importance of the forest in the Lele scheme of things:

> The prestige of the forest is immense. The Lele speak of it with almost poetic enthusiasm. God gave it to them as the source of all good things. They often contrast the forest with the village. In the heat of the day, when the dusty village is unpleasantly hot, they like to escape to the cool and dark of the forest . . . For going into the forest they use the verb *nyingena*, to enter, as one might speak of entering a hut, or plunging into water, giving the impression that they regard the forest as a separate element.[11]

There are three reasons, according to Douglas, for the great prestige of the forest: it is the source of subsistence, in the form of food, drink, building materials and clothes; it is the source of sacred medicines, necessary to the prophylaxis and treatment of natural and supernatural ills; and it is the scene of the hunt, 'which in Lele eyes is the supremely important activity'.[12]

Douglas leaves us in no doubt that the great utilitarian significance of the forest to the Lele as a source of the material means of life is only a part, and a subsidiary part, of its meaning for them. Its primary significance is religious. Its full meaning emerges when the forest and the symbolic world which Lele construct out of its wild denizens are set in the context of the total Lele universe.

The forest is the proper habitat of animals. Domestic animals appear to Lele as essentially anomalous. They have a fable which tells how a jackal and a partridge, the ancestors of dogs and poultry, came to throw in their lot with man. Ever since they have been continually begged by their forest kin to leave the human world and return to their natural home. 'For rats, which infest the huts of humans, Lele feel nothing but disgust. In conformity with their attitude to other anomalous animals, they never eat dog, domestic rats, or mice, and women extend the avoidance to a number of other rats and to all poultry.'[13]

Lele profess to be revolted at the idea of eating animals reared in the village. Although they nowadays breed pigs and goats, these are not for home consumption but for sale to customers of other tribes. 'Good food, they say, should come out of the forest, clean and wholesome, like antelope and wild pig.'[14]

At first sight it appears odd that Lele, who devote themselves to rule-governed interaction with such intensity, should also submit themselves so passionately to the particularly chancy business of hunting. But its seeming fortuity is for them the whole point. The result of a hunt cannot be calculated in advance. But according to Lele belief it is not random either. The success or failure of every hunting expedition is controlled by the spirits (*mingehe*). But their interventions are in no sense capricious. They withhold or deliver the animals according to the moral state of the hunting community.

Hunting is the only occasion, apart from the sporadic inter-village wars, when all the able-bodied men of a village act in concert. Otherwise they work alone, occasionally assisted by an age-mate or brother. Douglas emphasizes how the close physical proximity of individuals in the delicately balanced village society (even the hut walls are so thin that occupants can and do carry on conversations through them) is facilitated by a conventional requirement that men comport themselves in a suave, unaggressive manner. But in the forest outward appearances count for nothing. Before a communal hunt it the duty of every man to declare any animosity he might secretly harbour against a neighbour and to promise to let it rankle no more. Otherwise the spirits would see to it that the expedition was in vain.

When people quarrelled, they said, the forest went hard, no game came to the hunters' arrows or traps, the people suffered. Diviners could put it right with ritual, but not before the disputants had paid a fine. . . . Men liked to go to the hunt confident of their standing with one another, all grievances aired and settled. Their regular pre-hunting surveys of faults and omissions built up the sense of community. What is striking about the Lele is not how often they quarrelled, but how much it worried them when they did.[15]

If the first two or three draws of a hunting expedition produced no game, the men might hold another meeting and go through a ritual of appeasement: 'Two men would exchange weapons in the name of disputants, known or unknown, so that the hunt could proceed in good heart to the next draw.'[16]

The result of a hunt is taken by Lele as a reliable indicator of the state of their community. For it reveals, through the agency of the spirits, what is concealed in the ordinary way of things: man's inner self. Moreover it is a collective reality that is tested here, not the carefully controlled public face of the competitive individual but the hidden, spontaneous heart of man's communal being. Lele show by the supreme importance they assign to the forest in their scheme of things that it is this secret, anarchic heart of man-in-relation-to-his-fellows that they regard as of primary importance in life, not the minutely rule-governed *persona* of the visible social world. Yet these two disparate aspects of Lele existence, these realms which are apparently so mutually alien and disjunctive, are in fact interdependent and make up an integrated totality. The two worlds are mediated by the spirits.

No one has ever seen the *mingehe*. They live in the darkest depths of the forest, a region farthest removed physically from the neatly defined and subdivided village, standing in open and relatively elevated ground. Because the deep forest was also where the streams lay on which Lele relied for water, there was a close connection in Lele thought between water and the spirits. Certain animals which frequent the streams, such as the bush pig and water antelope, are regarded as highly charged with spiritual power and therefore dangerous unless proper ritual precautions are taken. Fish have to be handled with special care for the same reason.

As well as water, the spirits are also associated with night, the time when they are awake and roaming about the forest. Certain bush bucks are classed as 'spirit animals' (*hut a ngehe*) because they are active at night and so is the antelope (*cephalophus grimmi*).* A habit of sleeping in holes in the ground also associates an animal with the *mingehe*.[17]

Certain men understand the ways of the spirits. These are the diviners. Consideration of their qualifications and privileges finally confronts the investigator with the ambiguous actualities of the Lele universe. We already know it as one in which the component elements, both social and environmental, are rigorously separated and categorized. The final insight reveals separation and fragmentation as the obverse of an extraordinarily far-reaching integration.

Two of the cult groups, the Begetters and the Pangolin Men, have membership criteria that ensure that only elder men are eligible. The Begetters' group is composed of men who have fathered a child of either sex in wedlock; these must already be men of mature years, because the privileged position of the elders prevents the younger men from marrying. There is also a prolonged and expensive course of initiation which has a further restrictive effect. Membership of the Begetters' cult seems to have been important not so much for its own sake, but because it was a necessary first step to membership of a still more exclusive group, that of the Pangolin Men (*Bina Luwawa*). Begetters had no divining power, but they did have the right to eat the chest of any game and the meat of all young animals. To be eligible for admission to the Pangolin cult, a man had to have begotten a child of either sex by a wife who must be a member of one of the

---

* The Lele have a story that this animal sleeps during the day with eyes wide open: reinforcing the idea of oddity which seems to be associated with creatures the Lele regard as 'spirit animals'.

village's founding clans. In addition the candidate had to be himself a member of one of the founding clans, and likewise his father. These multiple conditions restricted membership of the cult to a select few in any village; sometimes there might be no one eligible.

Apart from these two cults whose membership was composed of men who had voluntarily decided to be initiated into them, there were other cult groups which were supposedly constituted by the direct intervention of the spirits. The largest of these was composed of men who had received a summons from the spirits in the form of a dream or a possession frenzy. Douglas remarks of this group that in spite of its theoretically involuntary recruitment, admission to it seemed to depend entirely on sponsorship by a father or a mother's brother.[18] The noviceship was arduous and costly. Another sign of a diviner's vocation was begetting twins. This was the only cult to which women as well as men were admitted. A third, very small group was that of the so-called 'diviners of God', who were supposed to be in direct contact with the spirits. A 'diviner of God' was exceptional in undergoing no initiation ceremony. Douglas describes him as 'a solitary, ascetic figure . . . he was held to be a diviner with at least as much power over spirits as the Pangolin Man'.[19]

The two essential matters over which the spirits had control were the disposition of game, as has been seen, and the fertility of women. These are both spheres which are beyond the control of conscious human intention. They are at the same time realms of activity which are fundamentally opposed in Lele culture. Fertility, an attribute of women, is the ultimate value in the book-keeping game in which Lele are involved as calculating, rational individuals. It is the productive power of women which is at stake in the intricate network of pawnship rights and obligations. Yet this ultimate value which is the 'object of the game' is outside the direct control of the contestants. The autonomy of women as self-acting human beings in a society which pretends to treat them as objects poses a similar contradiction:

A man's position depended on his control over women, but women were not so easy to coerce. Their action was much freer than Lele institutions, described from the male point of view, would imply. It was not impossible for a woman to end a marriage which did not

33

please her. If she transferred her attentions to one of her husband's brothers her preference would be hard to resist. If she favoured a man of another clan, fighting might ensue; men might be killed, but not she. If she ran away to another village, her husband would be prevented from reclaiming her by the armed force of the whole village which had given her refuge . . . When they considered that all their complex status system was built on such an uncertain basis, men would make a wry expression, saying: 'Women! Women! What can we do about them?'[20]

The contradiction found yet a third expression at the cognitive level where women were regarded at once as contemptible beings, approaching the low status of animals in their relative lack of 'shame' (*buhonyi*) as compared to the self-control and self-respect of men, and also as peculiarly weak and vulnerable (whence the elaborate prohibitions designed to shield them from contact with symbolically inappropriate foodstuffs).

All these apparent contradictions found a precarious resolution at a deeper level: the cosmological principle which assigned to all these concerns of the Lele village life a subordinate role when compared with the primacy of the forest. Here the world of wild nature mirrored in its rigorous, cross-cutting and balanced divisions the delicately counterposed sections of the village community. The forest, in contrast to the village with its equivocal feminine presence, was pre-eminently the preserve of men (though here too a contradiction lurked; as Douglas points out, the Lele economy would collapse without the labour that women performed in the forest. But their inferior status there was emphasized by regulations excluding them from the forest on every third day and on a number of special occasions, such as menstruation and childbirth).[21]

The communal hunt, as Douglas says, is a kind of spiritual barometer whose rise and fall is eagerly watched by the entire village.[22] It is the diviners who interpret the results of a hunt and prescribe what measures need to be taken in the frequent event of partial or total failure. Their prescriptions emphasize the primacy of forest over village, hunting over fertility, male over female. Before every hunt, the spokesman-treasurer, voicing the decision of the elderly village 'establishment', prohibits sexual intercourse the previous night. This ban may be extended if the hunt fails. Female fertility, the highest value in the competitive life of the Lele as individuals, is clearly subordinated to the communal value symbolized in the hunt. Moreover, success in the hunt is expected to ensure fertility in the village wives.

It is impossible not to be struck by the way in which child-bearing and hunting are coupled together, as if they were equivalent male and female functions. A village which has had a long series of bad hunts will begin soon to remark how few pregnancies there have been lately, or a village suffering from an epidemic or frightened by a recent series of deaths will send for a diviner to do medicine for them, saying that the village is spoilt, hunting has failed, women are barren, everyone is dying. Diviners themselves do not confuse the two symptoms. They perform distinct medicines for the separate disorders, but the grateful village whose hunting has been set on a sound basis will praise the medicine, saying, for example: 'Our village is soft and good now. Since the diviner went home we have killed three wild pigs and many antelopes, four women have conceived, we are all healthy and strong.'[23]

Each village appoints two men of different age groups (another instance of the pervasive dualism) to act as its official diviners. These men have the particular duty of countering sorcery.

What is a sorcerer? The Lele have a vivid image of this sinister person. In Douglas's rendering of it, 'he had broken kinship with mankind, and made it with the wild beasts. He ate no animal meat, only the putrefying flesh of human victims. While he existed in a village no enterprise could prosper. For jealousy of their happiness he killed small children. He envied the young and strong, and blighted them too. He polluted the water-supply. He "poisoned" the hunters' whetstones, blunted their arrows, in animal form he ran before them and saved their quarry.'[24]

Here is a threat to society which is far more sharply defined than the generalized lack of good will which is the most usual reason given, as we have seen, when a communal hunting expedition fails. In the sorcerer, what was implicit and collective is explicit, conscious and individualized. The sorcerer is the competitive, calculating individual of ordinary, legitimate Lele society realized in the counterposed, communal and spiritually superior world of the forest. Appropriately, the sorcerer assumes the form of a leopard, the most dangerous to man of all forest animals.

No one becomes a sorcerer's victim unless he has already been betrayed by a kinsman: 'If no clansman gives leave for you to be

35

killed, the weapons of the sorcerer fly by you, harmless. You cannot be killed if your clan all want you to live – except by God.'[25] Those who have been so betrayed become the sorcerer's familiars, in the shape of carnivorous animals called *mikadi*. In this form, inspired by hatred and a desire for revenge, they seek to kill their betrayers. Unless regularly supplied with fresh human victims by their master they will kill him too. So, as the Lele see it, a failure of love, death, hatred and retribution are linked in a terrifying causal chain. Such a prospect would be impossibly hard to bear without adequate defences against the active agents of evil, the sorcerers. Fortunately, Lele society also produces specialists who are able to meet the sorcerers on their own ground. The *ilumbi*, the official diviner, has skill in ritual and medicine equal to the sorcerer's; like him, he can assume the form of a leopard and rampage through the forest. His nimble feline intelligence is a match for the leopard-sorcerer and his train of vengeful familiars.

All may then be well, if a village is adequately protected by its official diviners. But there is always a suspicion that the *ilumbi* may turn out to be a double-agent, a sorcerer in disguise. This alarming possibility inheres in the fact that the skills of sorcerer and *ilumbi*, and indeed of all qualified diviners, are essentially the same. Lele tried to assure themselves of an *ilumbi*'s benevolence by obviating, as far as they could, possible sources of friction between him and the rest of the community. Adultery with one of his wives counted as an offence against the whole village, and the fine was correspondingly heavy. He on his part was denied access to village-wives* and could be fined if he broke this ban.

In the old days sorcery suspicions could be resolved one way or another by the administration of the poison ordeal, *ipome*. The rationale of the poison ordeal was that it found and put to the test the hidden inner being of a man. According to Lele doctrine, those who vomited the poison were innocent, while the guilty were unable to vomit and died. Since the proscription of the ordeal by the colonial authorities, Lele and many other African peoples have resorted to periodic anti-sorcery cults, in which 'medicine' is administered which is held to be automatically fatal to any who subsequently attempt to practice sorcery.

* Village-wives were women owned collectively by men of the younger age-sets, who were usually without 'private' wives.

It is the nature of such exotic cults to be transitory, passing fashions in ritual practice which are inevitably brought into disrepute by the persistence of social conflict. Their main function seems to be as a surrogate for the gap created in the community's mystical defences by the banning of the poison ordeal.[26] A return to the proven ways of Lele custom follows the abandonment of each discredited cult.

The implications of the dual nature of man as autonomous individual and social being are thoroughly explored in Lele culture. What that culture ultimately asserts is the unity of man's spirit. It endlessly divides, separates and classifies only to bind into a more cohesive whole. This seems to be the central meaning of the most exclusive and prestigious of all the Lele diviners' cults, that of the pangolin, or scaly ant-eater (*manis tricuspis*).

'. . . the pangolin was always spoken of as the most incredible monster of all. On first hearing it sounded such a fantastic beast that I could not believe in its existence,' writes Douglas.[27] The pangolin is of course a 'spirit animal' *par excellence*. Lele describe it as having the body and tail of a fish, being covered in scales. But it also has four legs and is given to climbing trees. It has other and more striking behavioural peculiarities. It suckles its young, which are brought forth singly, as in normal human birth, and quite unlike the multiple births typical of other animals. Perhaps most remarkable of all, the pangolin neither runs away from man, as most animals do, nor does it attack him. Instead it quietly curls up in a ball.

The pangolin is clearly the most anomalous of all the forest creatures, in terms of Lele categories. It appears to be a creature of the water, the element of the spirits, yet it walks and climbs on land. This apparent displacement from what should be its rightful habitat already charges the animal with spiritual power, as fish out of water are charged. Its manner of giving birth is more human than animal, and its apparently willing acceptance of death at the hands of man suggests a kind of consciousness unlike that of other creatures. The Lele indeed honour the dead animal, when it is being made ready for ritual eating by members of the pangolin cult, hailing it with the title of chief. 'Like Abraham's ram in the thicket and like Christ, the pangolin is spoken of as a voluntary victim. It is not caught, but rather it comes to the village. It is a kingly victim . . .'[28]

The pangolin, as Douglas says, is peculiarly apt because of its anomalous characteristics to play a mediating role between the opposed spheres of village and forest. This fundamental contra-position of the world of humanity and the world of wild nature is, we would argue, itself a metaphor expressing Lele awareness of a polarity in man's being between an individual, conscious and competitive self and a communal, preconscious and cooperative self.

But to leave it at that would be to miss the essence of Lele experience. For this is a people who are asserting integration and wholeness, precisely *through* division and separation. Every dimension of their universe carries this double imprint of dis-junction and unity: the rigid separation and interdependence of the sexes, the cross-cutting divisions of village society and the homologous cross-cutting classifications of the animal world.

Professor Douglas insists on the inter-relatedness of the three realms of village, forest and spirits: 'Lele religion is based on certain assumptions about the interrelations of humans, animals, and spirits. Each has a defined sphere, but there is interaction between them. The whole is regarded as a single system.'[29]

Lele maintain the delicate coexistence of multiplicity and integration by setting the centre of gravity of their society outside itself: by establishing the primacy over the open, rule-governed world of village society of the dark forest, the realm of the un-predictable spirits, whose disposition is none the less an un-relentingly impartial reflection of man's secret, communal being. The rite of the pangolin is only the most explicit expression of the pervasive ethos of ultimate oneness.

The complex unity of the Lele universe contrasts with the sim-ple dichotomy experienced by the Nuer, for whom the worlds of God and man are fundamentally distinct; their intermittent con-tact is primarily a matter for remedial measures, not celebration.[30] One might guess that the Lele pay a high price in personal hap-piness for their sense of ultimate cosmic integration. Not for them the gaiety of the Nuer herdsman singing the splendour of his oxen. They approach poetic language, it would seem, only when talking about the forest, with its hosts of ambiguous por-tents; or sometimes about women, who in other contexts are cause of grave and probably justifiable anxiety.[31]

The Lele achievement of integration through rigid separation has a parallel in modern Western experience. The complex inter-dependence wrought by extreme occupational specialization is an economic counterpart to a division and interrelatedness whose basis is primarily cognitive. Classification, the necessary prelude to all science, provides for the Lele not only a structural but a dynamic principle, for it sets them a puzzle which they can never solve, without bringing the house down. The evidence suggests that this people of the Congo forests have experienced and articulated something remarkably akin to the psychic dilemma of modern industrial society, simultaneously exposed to the actualities of individual isolation and the subordination of individuality to the needs of the collectivity.

3   Animal Classification and the Image of the Universe

The analysis of classification systems in non-literate societies is a persistent theme in the anthropology of Lévi-Strauss, and it has provided Mary Douglas with the key problems in *Purity and Danger*, a work which has already become an anthropological classic. Here we are concerned with the particular problem of the relation of animal classification to the structure of social experience, starting from the hypothesis that the ways in which different peoples categorize the external world are intimately related, in a manner yet to be determined, to the way in which each people perceives psycho-social reality.

Such a formulation of the problem leads us to posit the existence of certain basic premisses or predispositions which are logically prior to the classification schema. Our object is to elicit these basic premisses from a systematic comparison of the categories through which each society or culture apprehends the universe. This process of discovery is discontinuous rather than discursive, proceeding through cumulative exchanges of perspective which arise out of the dialectical logic inherent in the anthropological method.

We have seen that the world of wild animals is conceived by Nuer as a kind of mirror-image of human social organization, and relations with that world express what we have called a segmented consciousness of political events, or history.*

For Lele the symbolic implications of the animal classification schema are more profound: its cross-cutting categories not only

---

* There is a curious formal resemblance between the structure of Nuer social classification and the Western-scientific taxonomy of animate Nature: corresponding to the hierarchical nesting of kingdom, order, family, species and so on of the Linnaean scheme the Nuer has his clan and his maximal, major, minor and minimal orders of segmentation.

provide a formal mirror-image of each self-contained village society, thus resembling the Nuer example, but the system is also part of a unitary moral order pervading the whole universe – human, animal and spiritual.

We must now come to grips with our third example, the Fipa of south-west Tanzania, among whom the author lived for nearly two years.* What impresses him immediately is that classification possesses for the Fipa neither the basic organizational significance which it has for the Nuer, nor the deep cosmological significance it has for the Lele. By comparison with these two societies the Fipa appear to display a remarkable insouciance about taxonomic problems in general. The implications of this fundamental difference in attitude, as it now appears, will be progressively explored in later chapters in terms of its relation to a specific Fipa world-view.† With this end in mind, we need first to acquaint ourselves with the basic facts of Fipa social organization and with Fipa ideas about animals and animal classification.

Like the Lele, the Fipa belong to the great linguistic family of Bantu-speakers, whose numerous branches extend over one third of the African continent. They inhabit rolling and largely treeless uplands near the south-eastern shore of Lake Tanganyika. Their settlement pattern has some resemblance to that of the Lele, huts being densely concentrated in clusters which are relatively isolated one from another. The layout of each settlement, or village, appears less orderly than in the typical Lele settlement, with its neat grouping of huts reflecting the oppositions and alliances of age-sets. Fipa huts tend to be scattered higgledy-piggledy, except in larger settlements along the main roads where government authority has imposed a Western linearity on the builders. The overall plan tends to be circular, as against the rectangular boundaries of the Lele village. The huts themselves are rectilinear, with sloping roofs. This architectural style is an innovation, introduced during the colonial period; traditional Fipa huts were round, with a concentric interior corridor and a conical roof.

* From 1962 to 1964 and again in 1966. Fieldwork during the first period was financed through a generous grant from the Emslie Horniman Anthropological Scholarship Fund, and a return visit was made possible by the generosity of the Wenner-Gren Foundation for Anthropological Research.
† See especially pp. 123-124.

The Fipa are primarily agriculturalists, cultivating millet as a staple crop. They also keep a fairly wide range of livestock: cattle, goats, chickens and a few sheep and domesticated pigeons. Each village has its own headman, elected by the adult male residents from among their number;* the office is not hereditary nor, as commonly in Africa, is there a concept of association between descent groups and land, so that, where this association is found, one may speak of a particular lineage 'owning' a village. There is in fact no lineage system of the type which the Nuer exemplify, nor even a clan system of the residual Lele kind, where interrelated 'clan sections' are distributed between different villages. There are no named descent groups, with the exception of the royal dynasty, the Twa. The extended family (*uluko*) is an organization concerned exclusively with the inheritance of widows and wealth. It has no other social function.

Instead of a formal age-set system, villagers are classified simply by sex and according to age: as children, youngsters, mature men and women, and old people. There are no collective initiation ceremonies.†

The smallest unit of Fipa social organization is the nuclear household of husband, wife and children. But the most important unit is the village, *unnsi*, a residential and cooperative collectivity. Villagers form a moral community with a strongly egalitarian flavour. Joint working parties are the rule at times of most intensive effort in the fields – harvesting and threshing – although at other times men work alone in their plots, assisted only by their wives and unmarried children. All villagers are expected to participate in important ceremonies affecting any of their fellows, such as those of birth, marriage and death.

In pre-colonial times the villages of Ufipa‡ were grouped in two state systems, ruled by rival and related dynasties, called Twa. The Twa in both states considered the village headmen as forming the lowest tier in their administrative and tribute-col-

---

* Since 1965 the traditional office of village headman has been superseded by that of branch chairman of the Tanzanian governing party TANU (Tanzanian African National Union), elected by adult male and female suffrage.

† In pre-colonial times boys and girls had their two lower incisor teeth knocked out at puberty. This custom has not been observed for many years.

‡ Ufipa is the name given to the country of the Fipa.

lecting structure.* Both ruling lines base their claim to legitimacy on a myth according to which power was granted to them by the aboriginal chief of the country, whose descendant and present heir still reigns over a mountain enclave in central Ufipa. This tiny chiefdom, called Milansi ('the eternal village') is believed to have been founded by the first man in the world, called Ntatakwa ('the unnamed one'). These and cognate myths provide Fipa with some sense of ultimate common identity, transcending political and social divisions.

An anthropologist approaching a strange society tries to 'get into' it by learning its rules, patterned sets of ideas and attitudes (called 'institutions') on which the social system is based. When the inherent logic in these patterned sets has been adequately demonstrated, the anthropologist can claim to have 'understood' and 'explained' the exotic society. He and we can 'see how it works'. So an exploration of the implications of patrilineal descent revealed the social and political system of the Nuer; and the structure of oppositions and alliances formed by Lele age-sets explained the fragile cohesion of their village communities. Neither of these institutional devices is present in the Fipa case, so the logic of their social order has to be sought elsewhere than in a set of formal rules. Here we are up against a real and formidable problem of anthropological explanation.

The analytical categories so far developed in this book can give us a start towards the solution of this problem. How far do relations between human and animal worlds among the Nuer and Lele suggest a basis for comparison with the Fipa?

Nuer see their most valued domestic animals, cattle, as linked in a symbolic union with human society; this union has economic, emotional and cognitive aspects. Cattle provide the material means of life to the Nuer; they are a source of profound affective satisfaction; and, through the system of colour classification which associates the names of individual Nuer with aspects of nature, they relate men to the external environment. Nuer experience of integration with the cosmos is solitary and mediated through cattle. The lone herdsman composing songs in praise of his ox, his sweetheart and his kinsmen is the type figure of this culture.

---

* Under the British policy of 'indirect rule' this formal structure survived until 1962, when 'traditional' office-holders were deprived of political and legal status by the government of independent Tanganyika.

The world of wild animals is by contrast a distant one. The Nuer disdains hunting and feels that wild creatures inhabit a world apart from human society; he imagines its conformation as formally parallel in its ramifying groups to his own; the only relationship possible between humans and wild animals is that which associates individuals and groups with animal species in bonds of the greatest mutual respect (*thek*); such relationships are extraordinary by definition in that they are the product of extraordinary events.

For the Lele on the other hand it is domestic animals that are regarded with disdain, whereas hunting is the most prestigious occupation possible. While for the Nuer it is anomalous events that create relationships with wild species, for the Lele significant events (conception, success in hunting) are pre-eminently associated with one paradigmatically anomalous animal, the pangolin. The pangolin cult concentrates in one quintessential expression the significant elements of a complex of beliefs and attitudes which binds the whole social world of the Lele, as a totality, to the world of wild animals in a close relationship of dependence. This world is elaborately structured in Lele thought in a way that mirrors their own social order. Its boundaries and subdivisions are honoured in rigid dietary prohibitions applying to Lele women, supposedly the section of Lele society most vulnerable to the effects of symbolically inappropriate food. Nuer also observe dietary prohibitions, most particularly as an integral part of the *thek* relationship between both individuals and specific groups and animal species. But whereas for the Nuer the observation commemorates the unique individuality of a human being or a descent group (and is specially the concern of men), the restrictions observed by Lele women affirm the total interdependence of all members of the community.

The Fipa differ from both Nuer and Lele in important respects. Explicit dietary prohibitions have little part in their culture. Women were formerly supposed to eat neither chicken nor eggs, on the ground that these foods would make them sterile. Whether this prohibition was ever taken seriously I am not sure, but it is freely ignored nowadays. Members of the almost extinct Twa dynasty traditionally avoid sheep, chicken, guinea-fowl and all fish.* These rules, like Twa endogamy and the use of a special

---

* Another version of this taboo says that Twa may eat all fish except the black mudfish, *ikaambaale*.

language to describe royalty, presumably served to emphasize the special and exclusive identity of the Twa group as against Fipa commoners.

Otherwise there are few explicit rules. Chicken has highest prestige as a food, and is customarily offered to honoured guests. The meat of other domesticated animals – cattle, goat and pigeon – ranks next in order of preference. Dogs are not eaten, perhaps because of their scavenging habits but also because they are credited with providing early warning against human and animal intruders. They are useful creatures, and unsentimentally valued as such. The Fipa dog, *isiimbwa*, is not the focus of anything like the strongly emotive connotations of *mbwa*, 'dog', among the Lele.[1]

When home-reared meat is not available Fipa will satisfy their hunger with whatever wild flesh there may be; most often they are obliged to content themselves with their staple diet of millet porridge garnished with Lima beans. Hunters on the plateau occasionally shoot wild pig, antelope and bush buck, and their meat is relished. Traps yield hare, rats and moles, and these are also eaten. The author has seen a small carnivore, *ipiimbi*, resembling a weasel or mongoose, killed and eaten. Wild cats are held to be unsavoury and rejected except for medicinal purposes,* but this avoidance may be related to the belief that sorcerers dress in their skins. Certain wild birds and fish complete the diet.

The Fipa attitude to domestic animals falls halfway between the intense attachment of Nuer to their cattle and the qualified antipathy felt by Lele. It can best be described as utilitarian. Cattle and other livestock are regarded as different forms of wealth, with no symbolic value.† Cattle are rarely the victims in ritual sacrifice, and chickens and goats are the usual offerings.‡ But if domestic animals arouse in ordinary Fipa nothing of the fervour of a Nuer apostrophizing his favourite ox, there is little trace of the Lele 'contempt'. Good-humoured tolerance is suggested by the pet-

---

* See below, pp. 92–93. In general Fipa seem not to eat animals and birds used for ingredients in magical medicine.

† Exception must again be made of the Twa, for whom possession of cattle is, or was, an index of high social status. A milk-drinking ceremony was formerly a daily occurrence at the Twa court.

‡ The Twa are said to have sacrificed an ox in time of grave economic or political crisis, and the supreme tutelary spirit of Ufipa, Itweelele, is said to have occasionally required the sacrifice of a cow.

names 'Old Scratcher', applied to chicken, and 'Old Fusspot' and 'Old Shitter-at-God',* applied to goat. There seem to be no pet-names for dog or cattle, and it may be relevant that it is just these creatures, together with the generic term 'animal', which are frequently invoked as insults. Not however in the earnest manner of the Lele ('To call him a dog and tell him to go and eat excrement like a dog, that is the deadly insult, for which a man will try to kill his defamer')[2] but in the licensed ribaldry of cross-cousins or in the similarly licensed vituperation Fipa women sometimes employ against their lovers.† Even the house-rat evokes no special animosity, unlike the 'disgust' recorded for the Lele.[3] Fipa look upon them and mice, together with those small reptiles and insects which are wont to invade their living quarters, as part of the everyday scene. They will sometimes kill small animals and insects in their huts, but from impatience rather than fear or anger. Two insects enjoy a special immunity, at least as far as women are concerned. The praying mantis is believed to have the power to break cooking pots if it is killed,‡ and the appearance of a spider is supposed to be an omen of conception. Generally, peaceful coexistence of human and animal life, un-marked by strong emotion, is the rule in the village.

A comparable neutrality underlies the conventional Fipa attitude to the world of wild animals. Again there is, on the one hand, neither the detachment of the Nuer nor, on the other, the intense involvement of the Lele, but a businesslike appreciation of the profits and dangers to be found in the bush. Hunting is in general a secular activity which is neither disdained nor invested with a mystical prestige. The only category of hunters who en-joyed a special status in pre-colonial times were the elephant hunters, who formed a closed corporation with an elaborate body of magical lore.§ Hunting was occasionally endowed with sym-

---

* *Kanyeel'Indaaka.* The exposed anus of the goat, open to the sun (*In-daaka*), emblem of the otiose high God of the Fipa, is the object of this epithet. The name may also be applied to one who speaks foolishly, 'shooting his mouth off' to little purpose.

† Convention forbids Fipa men to reply in like manner (except in the case of cross-cousins), which is almost the reverse of Lele custom, according to which 'a man can with impunity and regularly does, call his wives "beasts, dogs"'.

‡ It is called by a name meaning 'pot-breaker'.

§ A man who belonged to this corporation was distinguished by the title

bolic significance when a decision had to be reached, in pre-colonial times, on the siting of a new village. Villagers went on a collective hunt and if the first animal taken was female, it was interpreted as a sign that the local spirits approved of the project, while a male animal meant disapproval.

Normal hunting is solitary, when a man goes into the bush accompanied by one or more dogs.* It is a utilitarian activity. The hunter carries a long bow and a handful of poisoned arrows, and a spear to defend himself against attack by big game. Fipa animal classification reflects a practical concern with speedy identification of the inhabitants of their natural environment. It has the following form:

	Fipa term
All land animals (both domestic and wild, and including all reptiles except snakes)	inyama
All game animals	inkala *or* amayiinga
All dangerous wild land animals	ifikaangu
Birds	ifyuuni
Snakes	amasoka
Fish	inswi
Insects	ifyoongoli

I found no evidence that the Fipa regarded animals which resisted assimilation to their basic taxonomy as disturbing or symbolically significant. Rather the contrary, as suggested by this light-hearted fable on the problem of classification posed by the bat:

Long ago the birds fought a war against the land animals. At first the animals were winning, and so Bat came forward and announced: 'I am an animal, and not a bird. Look at my teeth, and my ears!'

But in the end the birds beat the animals. Then Bat appeared again, and said: 'But I am a bird, not an animal. Can an animal fly?'

In the end the birds and the animals agreed together to drive out

---

of *umwaami*, 'master'. Similar corporations, which may have been composed mainly of Sukuma migrants from northern Tanzania, monopolized the hunting of snakes and porcupines, respectively.

* It may be significant that the verb *ukusowa*, meaning to hunt collectively, using nets, also has the meaning 'to act foolishly, without sense'.

Bat. So now he hides himself in a cave and comes out only at night, so as not to be seen.

This unconcern about the cognitive boundaries formed by category discriminations, this willingness to 'fudge' or transcend the boundaries in the interest of a more inclusive grasp of the total range of phenomena, is common to both the social and natural worlds of the Fipa. But because a common attitude informs Fipa perception of both social and natural worlds does not mean that in the Fipa case we are dealing with two homologous structures, as in the juxtaposed and formally congruent social and feral worlds of the Nuer – there is no imagined array of 'village communities' in the domain of Fipa wild animals, no equivalent of the segmentary lineage structure attributed by Nuer to wild creatures.

Instead we find that Fipa perception of natural phenomena is structured by a single criterion, that of social relevance. Categories are provisional, subject to the overriding question of social significance, not meaningful in their own right as symbols of cosmic order, as among the Lele. With the Fipa, the source of order is located firmly within the human community as realized in the village settlement, not projected on to the unknown world outside the village, as in the Lele universe.

The master principle of Fipa animal classification emerges clearly from a consideration of Fipa ideas about the eland, *imbeesi*. This is the only animal in the Fipa bestiary, apart from the python, which is credited with mystical power such that no hunter would dare kill it without first immunizing himself with appropriate 'medicines'. Otherwise, it is said, the 'spirit' (*unnsimu*) of the animal would, in revenge, visit the hunter with grave and possibly fatal illness.

This evaluation of the eland is based on a particular combination of facts and attitudes. The various species of antelope are distinguished by Fipa according to names which reflect differences in the size and shape of their horns. This criterion is in turn based on a utilitarian consideration: the horns of the smaller antelopes are used by Fipa as containers for both beneficial and maleficent 'medicines', and are thus, in Fipa eyes, of pre-eminent utility.* The immense horns of the eland, largest of the ante-

* See pp. 91–95 for a discussion of the prime place of 'medicines' in the Fipa world view.

lopes, are, however, far too large to be employed for this purpose. The eland also differs from the other antelopes in being classified, realistically in view of its great size and strength and the destructive potential of its horns, as an *icikaangu*, an animal dangerous to man. The attribution of an injurious mystical power to the eland is thus a reflection of the dual fact that it is both dangerous to man in reality and, in the most important embodiment of that danger, its horns, appears to incarnate in alarmingly unmanageable form a feature of antelope morphology which in less intimidating members of the order men have turned to particularly useful account.

It would be fair to say that in Fipa consciousness there is little or no trace of any notion of a world of wild animals existing in its own right, a view that is explicit in Nuer thought and implicit in Lele animal symbolism. Those animals classified as *ifikaangu*, 'dangerous beasts', cut across taxonomic criteria of eating habits, morphology and habitat to embrace not only the large mammalian carnivores, lion, leopard and hyaena, but also the reptilian crocodile, king cobra and spitting cobra, and the herbivores, elephant, hippopotamus, buffalo and eland.

Only one animal is intrinsically symbolic for the Fipa, and that is the python, *insato*. In Fipa religion particular pythons were frequently identified with named territorial spirits, *imyaao nkaandawa*. These creatures and other pythons who might be encountered in the bush were customarily greeted with the title of kingship, '*Mweene*'.

Fipa folklore recognizes both a good, or positive, aspect of 'pythonhood' and an evil, negative aspect. The former occurs in the revered animals which incarnate the territorial spirits, and the latter in stories of dragon-like, anti-human creatures. One of these terrifying beasts is celebrated in a tale common in southern Ufipa under the name of Zimwi, 'Indeterminate Thing-ness' or 'Chaos'. Breathing fire from its nostrils and uttering strident cries it made the lives of the first men on earth a misery, instantly appearing as soon as they had killed some game and making off with their quarry. Zimwi was eventually killed by Mtanji, 'the Toolmaker', a culture hero who is said to have first shown men how to cultivate, make hoes and build traps.[4]

There is also a widespread story in Ufipa about a gigantic python-like beast called *Ingufwiila*, 'the Destroyer'. I was told it attained a length of about a hundred and twenty feet and was reddish in colour.* Even to see this horrendous animal is fatal to ordinary mortals, but its exceptional power (*amaaka*) can be harnessed by those experts in the manipulation of natural forces whom the Fipa call *asiŋaanga*, 'doctors'.†

Having first immunized himself with protective 'medicine' (*amaleembo*), the 'doctor' builds a small hut near the lair of Ingufwiila. Inside the hut he puts a live chicken, then seals the door. He then sets pointed stakes all round the hut, and retires to a safe distance. Sooner or later the cries of the chicken arouse Ingufwiila, who tries to encircle the hut and crush it in his coils. Instead he is impaled on the stakes and loses much blood before making off. After that the 'doctor' goes and collects the earth which is soaked in the blood of Ingufwiila, and it makes very powerful 'medicine'.

There seems to be a direct relation between Fipa unconcern with social and natural taxonomy, their lack of emotional investment in it, and the relative poverty of Fipa animal symbolism. The full meaning of the python in Fipa religion can emerge only after a more extended treatment of the Fipa world view, developed in later chapters of this book. For the moment it suffices to note that in the Fipa case we are dealing with a culture that is unashamedly pragmatic in its evaluation of the external world, including the domain of animals. Its judgements are answers to the question, What is the use of *that* to *us*, the human community? This utilitarian interest makes for a down-to-earth and somewhat irreverent attitude to wild animals, contrasting markedly with the respect accorded in principle to all wild life by the Nuer and the mystical aura projected on to the world of wild beasts by the Lele.

The Fipa attitude to the lion is symptomatic. Formally, there is an association between this animal and royalty, as evidenced by a complex of customs linking Twa chiefship and parts of the animal's body. Thus, at his installation ceremony, a Twa chief spins a twig in the hip-bone of a lion to make ritual fire, which is then used to rekindle extinguished hearths all over the country. The chief's appointed messengers and tribute gatherers wear armbands of lion-skin as insignia of authority. The royal regalia includes a ceremonial whistle trimmed with the tuft of a lion's

---

* In Fipa colour symbolism red is associated with violence and disorder.
† On these traditional specialists, see also below, pp. 91–95.

tail: the chief blows this whistle at night on retiring, after which there must be silence in the royal village until he blows it again in the morning.*

But this use of parts of the lion's body as emblems of royalty is not extended by Fipa to an assertion of equivalence between the abstract idea of the lion and chiefship. Dead Twa chiefs are reputed to become pythons, not lions. Only evil men called *aloosi*, sorcerers, are credited with the power of metamorphosing themselves into lions, and other dangerous animals; and sorcery is not an attribute of Fipa chiefship.

The very names given to the beast are half-humorous and mildly derogatory. *Kalaangu*, the most common term for lion, means literally 'big noise'; another term, *icisama*, means 'roaring thing' and there is a familiar or pet-name, *mbulukutu*, an onomatopoeic term which could be translated as 'Old Growler'. Reduced in this way to the status of an auditory nuisance, the lion is almost domesticated. In Fipa folk stories Lion is customarily cast in the role of an amiable idiot, no match, in spite of his physical strength, for the ruthlessness of Hyaena or the guile of Hare.

We now know enough of Fipa animal categories to see that we are dealing with a view of the universe which is both unitary, in contrast with the dual Nuer worlds of society and wild nature, and man-centred, in contrast to the Lele location of a cosmic centre of gravity outside the village, in the wild forest. But to reach the deep structure of that universe we must first retrace our steps and establish, for detailed comparison with the Lele and Fipa evidence, the key features of the Nuer cosmos.

* The reader should be cautioned that these statements about Fipa customs are made in the 'ethnographic present'. The customs lapsed quite early in the colonial period.

4   Twins, Birds and False Consciousness

Nuer thought is built round the theme of balanced opposition. Heaven and earth, Spirit and creation, human society, with its homologous bovine component, and wild nature: these are ideally separate, and their conjunction is an extraordinary, unfortunate or even tragic event. Nuer erect special shrines for those killed by lightning; sickness is directly or indirectly (as with ritual pollution)[1] attributed to the intervention of Spirit; and the founding of a new descent group is often celebrated retrospectively, as we have seen, by association with a wild creature.

But from another aspect, Nuer paradoxically assert that these ideal divisions are really flaws introduced into an originally integral and perfect state of peace and harmony, in which death, conflict, labour, sexual desire and hunger were all unknown. Earth was joined to heaven by a rope and anyone who became old climbed up to God, was rejuvenated and returned to earth.

One day a hyena – an appropriate figure in a myth relating to the origin of death – and what is known in the Sudan as a durra-bird, most likely a weaver bird, entered heaven by this means. God gave instructions that the two guests were to be well watched and not allowed to return to earth where they would certainly cause trouble. One night they escaped and climbed down the rope and when they were near the earth the hyena cut the rope and the part above the cut was drawn upwards towards heaven. So the connexion between heaven and earth was cut and those who grow old must now die . . .[2]

Another myth says that all creatures, including man, originally lived together in fellowship in one camp. Dissension began after Fox persuaded Mongoose to throw a club into Elephant's face. A quarrel ensued and the animals separated; each went its own way and began to live as they now are and to kill each other.

Stomach, which at first lived a life of its own in the bush, entered into man so that now he is always hungry. The sexual organs, which had also been separate, attached themselves to men and women, causing them to desire one another constantly. Elephant taught man how to pound millet so that he now satisfies his hunger only by ceaseless labour. Mouse taught man how to beget and woman how to bear. And Dog brought fire to man.[3]

Fox is also made indirectly responsible for another basic division in the Nuer cosmos, that between wild and domestic animals. He is said, while he was plotting to sow dissension among the animals, to have given man a spear and taught him how to use it.

> It was then that man began to kill, and his first killing seems to have been that of the mother of cow and buffalo, or rather the mother of cattle, for at that time cows and buffaloes were the same. This led to a feud between men and cattle, buffaloes avenging their mother by attacking men in the bush and cows by causing men to quarrel and slay one another.[4]

This theme of balanced duality in the Nuer cosmos has been interestingly extended by T. O. Beidelman. He claims to identify a conscious opposition in the Nuer psyche between the communal idea of agnatic solidarity and the individual's drive towards sexual and social domination over his fellows. These two opposed values are symbolically represented in Nuer thought as the contrast between the 'socialized' ox and the dominant, sexually aggressive bull. Beidelman concludes his stimulating re-analysis of the Nuer material, an analysis which seeks to complement rather than supersede the work of Evans-Pritchard, by stressing, in the case of these two incompatible values, the quality of balanced opposition we have already noted in other dimensions of Nuer thought:

> In the spearing of an ox a Nuer expresses a kind of transfiguration, through immolation, of his sexual self and an anticipation of his own transformation, through death, into the agnatic ideal person which his own living, domestic sexual self cannot wholly be and, indeed, cannot wholly accept. This is not to suggest that Nuer consider agnatic ideals the only important values in their society. It is their recognition of their deep personal commitment to domestic values which conflict with these ideals that leads them to focus ritual upon the ambiguous

53

tensions these cross-cutting values produce. The values of agnation are more inclusive and enduring than domesticity, but Nuer seem to recognize that these are less compelling in everyday life.[5]

Beidelman has here, in my view, accurately identified a basic structural *coupure* in the Nuer universe, and to that extent his analysis constitutes an important extension, in the psychological dimension, of Evans-Pritchard's account of Nuer social and cognitive categories. My only reservation concerns the force of the word 'sexual' in Beidelman's analysis. The history of anthropology bears witness to the imprudence of applying uncritically to non-Western societies descriptive concepts drawn from Western culture, and 'sexuality' is one of those concepts.*

With this reservation, I would gratefully accept Beidelman's characterization of the dualistic structure of the Nuer psyche, a characterization which is also entirely congruent with Evans-Pritchard's account. For Beidelman's critical exegesis of the Nuer ethnography enables us to confirm that in their inward conformation Nuer replicate the balanced dualism pervading the rest of their universe. We can now approach again, and to more purpose, a peculiarly Nuer concept which has been the subject of much learned controversy: the equation of human twins with birds.

Evans-Pritchard convincingly acquits the Nuer of irrational or 'prelogical' thinking in this context. A twin, he says, on account of his peculiar manner of conception, is taken by Nuer as a manifestation of Spirit (*Kwoth*). He is a 'child of God' (*gat kwoth*) and when he dies his soul goes into the sky, the principle abode of Spirit. He is a *ran nhial*, a person of the above, whereas an ordinary person is a *ran piny*, a person of the below. In this he resembles a bird, which belongs by nature to the sky and is also what Nuer call, using 'person' metaphorically, a person of the above, and is therefore also associated with Spirit. 'Birds are children of God on account of their being in the air, and twins belong to the air on account of their being children of God by the manner of their conception.'[6]

---

* This is not the place to develop this line of argument further, but I would contend that 'sex' has distinct, and distinctly different, meanings in Nuer, Lele, Fipa and Western culture, and that therefore the term 'sexual' needs to be carefully defined in each case and not used, as in this and certain other writings by T. O. Beidelman, as if it were in itself an explanatory concept.

Evans-Pritchard is saying that the twins–birds equation is based on an analogy between the relationship of both to God, relationships which are conceived of in the same terms. 'The formula does not express a dyadic relationship between twins and birds but a triadic relationship between twins, birds and God. In respect to God twins and birds have a similar character.'[7]

Lévi-Strauss has objected to the inclusion of God in this formulation: 'A belief in a supreme deity is not necessary to the establishment of relations of this type, and we have ourselves demonstrated them for societies much less theologically minded than the Nuer.'[8]

But his objection is beside the point. What we most need to know is not what metaphorical ideas of this kind have in common with those of a similar kind in other societies, but what the total significance of the cluster of ideas involved in the twins–birds equation is for the Nuer. In my view even Evans-Pritchard has not reached the heart of the matter. The resolution of the problem turns on two issues: the symbolic meaning of twinship and the esoteric significance of the incapsulation in a single formula of twins and birds.

Why, in Evans-Pritchard's words, is 'twin-birth a special revelation of Spirit'?[9] Evans-Pritchard implies that it is because the birth of twins is a relatively unusual event, and we have indeed seen that for Nuer all extraordinary happenings tend to be conceived of as manifestations of an external force, or spirit. But it is not its unusual character that suggests the analogy with birds, which are normal natural phenomena, but its association with Spirit. I suggest that this association primarily occurs because human twins are apt 'natural symbols' for the relation of balanced duality which we have seen to pervade all dimensions of the Nuer cosmos. They appear as two closely similar or identical physical beings. They are clearly separate but they were born at more or less the same time from the body of one woman. Nuer conceptualize the merging in twinship of the ideas of unity and duality by saying that twins, though two human beings, are one 'person' (*ran*). This social unity of twins is expressed in rituals connected with marriage and death, in which the social *persona* is changed. When the senior of male twins marries, the junior acts with him in the ritual he has to perform; female twins are supposed to be married on the same day; and no mortuary ceremony is held for a single twin because one of them cannot be cut off from the living without the other.[10]

These characteristics of the Nuer concept of twinship amount to an exact ideological template for the structural pattern informing their entire universe. Twins are physically separate and autonomous human beings. They are entirely distinguishable one from another. Yet for a twin the status of twinhood is defined in terms of another, who is defined in the same way in terms of himself. There is at one and the same time separation and unity of being in twinship. In just such a way are human and bovine society merged and opposed. As Beidelman remarks:

> There is a highly developed symbolic relation between Nuer and their cattle; they go through somewhat similar stages of development and, just as Nuer fall into social categories, such as children, women, adult men, influential adults (usually men), so, too, cattle fall into categories of calves, cows, oxen and bulls.[11]

The intimate interdependence of men and cattle has been described earlier, dramatically epitomized in the moment of ritual sacrifice when ox dies for man as his surrogate. Yet what Evans-Pritchard calls the 'identification' of man with cattle[12] implies also the clearest distinction and opposition between bovine and human. The parallel with twinship is exact: absolute distinction combined with an identification which implies that what is distinguished as two is also one, as Nuer speak of twins being two people but one person.

The same pattern emerges in the political dimension. Agnatic unity and segmentary division are two sides of the same coin, interdependent, balanced opposites.

> . . . the political system is an equilibrium between opposed tendencies towards fission and fusion, between the tendency of all groups to segment, and the tendency of all groups to combine with segments of the same order. The tendency towards fusion is inherent in the segmentary character of Nuer political structure, for although any group tends to split into opposed parts these parts must tend to fuse in relation to other groups, since they form part of a segmentary system. Hence fission and fusion in political groups are two aspects of the same segmentary principle, and the Nuer tribe and its divisions are to be understood as an equilibrium between these two contradictory, yet complementary, tendencies.[13]

We have noted the same reciprocal principle of balanced opposition appear in Nuer consciousness as the counterposed ideas of communal, agnatic solidarity and individual competitiveness and divisiveness, symbolized by the passive 'socialized' ox and the aggressively dominant bull. The first is the notion of unity, the second that of plurality, epitomized in duality, its simplest and most fundamental form. Nuer recognize that these two values, different and opposed as they are, are of equal importance, as Beidelman points out.

A much wider division separates human society, with its closely associated bovine simulacrum, from the similarly structured world of wild animals. We have seen that contact between these two distanced worlds constitutes a historical event in either the individual psyche, when a person acquires an animal totem, or in the social organization, when the founder of a descent group is imagined as born a twin to a wild animal. Here again, in the *thek* relationship of mutual respect which individuals and groups exceptionally have with wild species, the emphasis is on balanced opposition. The *thek* obligation is reciprocal and may be considered abrogated if the animal species is considered to have broken it.

Another friend, Rainen of the Leek tribe, told me that he used to respect lions because his paternal grandfather's mother had been born twin to a lion in Dinkaland (she was a Dinka), the lion twin having run away into the bush. He said, however, that he had ceased to respect them when they began to eat his cattle. . . . He said '*ce theak thuk*', 'the respect is finished'. The same man told me that in the past, before lions began to eat his cattle, he had sometimes tied up a goat in the bush for them, and they had taken it.[14]

On the grandest scale the Nuer conceive their universe as dicotomized between Spirit and creation, associated respectively with the sky and the earth. The immense contrast between these two opposed spheres is emphasized by Nuer, and by Evans-Pritchard in his account of their thought and attitudes. 'Nuer pathetically compare man to heavenly things. He is *ran piny*, an earthly person and, according to the general Nuer view, his ghost is also earthbound. Between God and man, between heaven and earth, there is a great gulf.'[15] Nuer picture themselves humbly as 'the ants of God' and in prayers to God they say, 'it is thine earth, it is thine universe'. Being earthbound they cannot mount up to God, but God can come to them, being everywhere, like wind and air.[16]

Evidence of the humility of Nuer in relation to their God, for which there is ample support in Evans-Pritchard, may give the impression that their lives are dominated by religion. Put thus simply, this would be no more than a half-truth. Nuer are ambivalent in their attitude to God: 'Nuer, like other people, want it both ways. They want God to be near at hand, for his presence aids them, and they want him to be far away, for it is dangerous to them.'[17]

For most of the time, indeed, except when sickness and other misfortunes compel them to seek divine help, Nuer seem to be happy to leave God alone with his own business and get on with theirs. Nuer humility before God may then be seen to contrast sharply with their arrogance towards their fellow man.

That every Nuer considers himself as good as his neighbour is evident in their every movement. They strut about like lords of the earth, which, indeed, they consider themselves to be. There is no master and no servant in their society, but only equals who regard themselves as God's noblest creation.[18]

Nuer consciousness of the omnipotence and omnipresence of God only heightens awareness of the gulf separating the worlds of Spirit and creation. On the one hand they constantly affirm the ultimate and fundamental unity of the cosmos, as the work of God. But on the other they know themselves as part of the created world, separated from God. Unity and duality paradoxically coexist, opposing interdependent and balancing principles, exactly as in the concept of twinship. Here Spirit and creation, the constituent principles of the cosmos, are related to each other analogously to the balanced and opposed interrelation, at the level of human society, between the normative concept of agnatic unity and the existential concept of individual competition.

The dialectic between aggressive individualism and communal fellowship is graphically described by Evans-Pritchard in the context of inter-personal relations among the Nuer.

The Nuer have rightly been described as dour, and they are often gruff and curt to one another and especially to strangers. But if they are approached without a suggestion of superiority they do not decline friendship, and in misfortune and sickness they show themselves kind and gentle. At such moments they permit themselves to show sympathy which their pride stifles at other times, for even when Nuer approve of one they cannot bear that one shall see it and are the more truculent to hide their friendliness. Never are they truckling or sycophantic. When a Nuer wants a gift he asks for it straight out, and if you refuse it he remains in good humour. Their only test of character is whether one can stand up for oneself.[19]

It should be apparent by now that a structural leitmotiv, which can be characterized as the paradoxical opposition and balance of unity and duality, links together the various dimensions of Nuer experience: psychic, inter-personal, political and cosmological. This leitmotiv, or 'template', is most cogently expressed in the Nuer concept of twinship, in which separate, equal and reciprocally distinguished and opposed individuals are conceived as participating in a single personality. But what is the meaning of the equation of twins with birds?

As well as being, as we have seen, an exact 'natural symbol' for this pervasive structural principle, human twins are also its nearest and most compact expression. These living embodiments of the interdependence of unity and duality are part of a Nuer's most immediate experience, the human society he lives in; and they were once indistinguishably part of the body of one human being, their mother. Birds, with which the formula contrasts and equates them, symbolize, in extreme contrast, the grandest and most inclusive 'twinlike' embodiment of unity and duality in the Nuer cosmos: the opposition and ultimate oneness of God and his creation, heaven and earth. Birds, especially those which fly high, 'seem to us as well as to Nuer, to belong to heaven rather than to earth and therefore to be children of light and symbols of the divine'.[20]

In this formula, birds represent one side of this grand cosmic opposition, that of Spirit. But *Kwoth*, as we have seen, is not only one side of the opposed worlds of God and his creation, he is also unity, the ultimate oneness of the universe. Just so, on earth, twins are both two and one. Fully elaborated, the twins–birds equation is saying that balanced opposition of unity and duality runs through the Nuer universe from its micro- to its macro-structure; and it is also saying that unity, represented by the symbolic term 'birds', is the dominantly valued aspect of twin-ship.*

The structure of Nuer consciousness seems admirably adapted to the simultaneous accommodation of integrative and divisive, synthetic and analytic, modes of apprehension, untroubled by any felt need to reconcile these antithetical modes in terms of a meta-theory. Further inquiry suggests that the theme of balanced opposition pervading the various dimensions of their psycho-social order is grounded in a social-relational dualism inherent in their predominantly pastoral economy.

Nuerland consists of a vast, flat and almost treeless plain, threaded with waterways which flood and turn most of the coun-try into swamp in the wet season; in the dry season most of the streams dry up, leaving only the large rivers, the Nile and its major tributaries. These harsh conditions compel the Nuer to make a twice-yearly migration, or transhumance: 'Nuer are forced into villages for protection against floods and mosquitoes and to engage in horticulture, and are forced out of villages into camps by drought and barrenness of vegetation and to engage in fishing.'[21]

This means that Nuer experience every year an alternation in span of social relations between the isolation of small village communities in the wet season and the much wider relations necessitated by the migrations and temporary settlement in the dry season camps, which accommodate members of many differ-ent villages.

> There may be wide dispersal of communities and low density of population, but there is seasonal contraction and wide interdepend-ence . . . Thus, on the one hand, environmental conditions and pas-toral pursuits cause modes of distribution and concentration that provide the lines of political cleavage and are antagonistic to political cohesion and development; but, on the other hand, they necessitate extensive tribal areas within which there is a sense of community and a preparedness to co-operate.[22]

The wider relations of interdependence set up during the dry season tend to create a sense of identity and common interests which can easily be transformed into organized and aggressive

* A solution of the problem of Nuer dualism is suggested in our concluding chapter, pp. 118-122.

expansion at the expense of other Nuer groups, or, as often in the past, of the pastoralist neighbours of the Nuer, the Dinka. According to Evans-Pritchard the Nuer have in this way conquered large areas of formerly Dinka territory since the middle of the nineteenth century, absorbing many Dinka groups into their own social organization in the process.[23] In contrast to, and in contradiction with, the wide-ranging corporate solidarity realized in this territorial expansion of the Nuer, their annual contraction into isolated villages re-creates social divisions and a sense of local exclusiveness. Each village is an economic corporation, owning its particular gardens, water supplies, fishing-pools and grazing grounds, and its own site in the dry-season camp.[24] What Evans-Pritchard calls the 'situational fission and fusion' of Nuer social groups has a basic paradigm in the yearly alternation, necessitated by the oscillating state of the natural environment, between a wide and a narrow span of social relations.

The universe of balanced duality Nuer have created can thus be seen as anchored in nature itself, or rather in the basic model of two-way change and relativity in social relations which the exigencies of a pastoralist way of life have imposed on them. This fact probably gives to Nuer social organization and ideology a degree of intrinsic strength and impermeability to outside influence which is lacking in societies which are economically based on a process of transformation of natural resources, like the agricultural Lele and Fipa. The inherent stability of the Nuer political and social system is suggested by the fact that equilibrium between the divisive and unifying tendencies has been unaffected by its aggressive expansion into Dinka territory. Indeed, according to a plausible argument by Professor Sahlins, it is precisely the situational operation of the fission and fusion principles which has enabled Nuer groups to colonize and hold land formerly occupied by the Dinka. In a competitive search for new pastures lineage heads lead their followers into foreign territory. When fighting ensues with the Dinka occupants the fusion principle operates to bring superior force to bear against the defenders, whose social organization is more loosely structured and lacks such a tendency to spontaneous cohesion.

After the predictable defeat of the fragmented Dinka the temporary Nuer consolidation breaks down into its component groups. Ambition leads some of them into new expansionist adventures, and the fusion principle can again work to Nuer advantage when they meet resistance. Sahlins concludes that the Nuer system of situational fission and fusion of political groups has evolved out of the need to expand into the territory of a numerically superior but less well-organized tribal neighbour.[25]

This account gives a satisfyingly objective explanation of an historical process which Evans-Pritchard seems to view, no doubt reflecting in part the opinions of his informants, as a proof of the superior courage and fighting spirit of the Nuer as compared with the contemptible Dinka:

> Nuer have a proper contempt for Dinka and are derisive of their fighting qualities, saying that they show as little skill as courage. *Kur jaang*, fighting with Dinka, is considered so trifling a test of valour that it is not thought necessary to bear shields on a raid or to pay any regard to adverse odds, and is contrasted with the dangers of *kur Nath*, fighting between Nuer themselves. These boasts are justified both in the unflinching bravery of the Nuer and by their military success.[26]

Evans-Pritchard goes as far as to speak of Nuer and Dinka as 'immemorial enemies'. Nearly always it is the Nuer who have been the aggressors. Raiding the Dinka is for Nuer 'a normal state of affairs and a duty' which is explained and justified by a myth. This describes how God promised his old cow to his son Dinka and his young calf to his son Nuer. Then Dinka came by night to God's byre, imitated the voice of Nuer and obtained the calf. 'When God found that he had been tricked he was angry and charged Nuer to avenge the injury by raiding Dinka's cattle to the end of time.'[27]

The aggressive expansion against the Dinka which this myth legitimizes for Nuer is so customary and permanent that Evans-Pritchard describes the two tribes as forming a single political system. 'Contiguous Dinka and Nuer tribes are segments within a common structure as much as are segments of the same Nuer tribe. Their social relationship is one of hostility and its expression is in warfare.'[28]

This relationship between Nuer and Dinka appears by its marked asymmetry (the Nuer almost invariably the aggressors, and frequently expanding territorially at the expense of the Dinka) to contradict the principle of balanced opposition which has been found to pervade the Nuer universe. As Sahlins puts it, the significance of Nuer aggression is that, while preserving equilibrium inside Nuer society, through the operation of situational fission and fusion, it disturbs equilibrium 'in the larger and more revealing perspective of the intercultural milieu'. The interesting question is how this structurally anomalous situation is accommodated to the dominant idiom of Nuer thought. Nuer society is one without history in the usual sense of a collectively conceptualized series of events, conceived as significant for the whole society. All that is retained of the past are events that can be inferred from the relation in the present of different lineage segments; from these relations, from what Evans-Pritchard calls 'structural distance', Nuer infer the relative time–distance since each group's foundation. This way of conceiving the past absorbs it into the social structure, rather as conquered Dinka groups are absorbed by fusion into Nuer social organization: 'when the balanced opposition between a Nuer political segment and a Dinka political segment changes into a relationship in which the Nuer segment becomes entirely dominant, fusion and not a class structure results'.[29]

It is characteristically through the image of twinship, but an *unequal* twinship, that Nuer conceive of their aggressive expansion into Dinka country. The idea of an ancestor born twin to a wild animal is, in Nuer symbolic imagery, specially apt to the founders of those Nuer descent groups which have colonized Dinka country. As always with such key concepts, several ideas are here consolidated in this dual image. There is twinship itself, the symbol of balanced opposition which is the structural basis of the Nuer cosmos; there is the negation of balance, the assertion of asymmetry, in the substitution of a wild creature for the counterposed human being; and the wild animal itself represents a world which is both alien to Nuer society but also cast in a similar structural mould, just as Nuer and Dinka 'are alike in their ecologies, cultures, and social systems, so that individuals belonging to the one people are easily assimilated to the other'.[30]

We can now venture to hazard an answer to a question which remained unanswered earlier. Why are certain Nuer lineages associated with the spirits of wild animals while others lack such associations? I suggest that it is those groups which have come into being through aggressive expansion into Dinka territory which wear this badge of unbalanced twinship. This conjecture seems to be lent some support by Evans-Pritchard's statement that 'many lineages have no totemic affiliations, and those who have them tend to be thought of as at one time not having them and of having *at some point in time and through some event* acquired them; and Nuer also tend to think of them as *something they got from the Dinka*'.[31]

After writing these words I came across a recent article by Kathleen Gough on Nuer kinship[32] in which a strikingly similar theory is presented by the author, albeit couched in somewhat different terms, to account for apparent anomalies in the Nuer kinship system in the area of Nuer expansion into Dinka territory. In this area, according to Gough, Nuer conquest of Dinka resulted in

a state of structural change such that the actual domestic relations of a large proportion of the population, especially with regard to male rights over women, do not fit the ideals of patrilineal descent, but are nevertheless continually reinterpreted, through a series of *customary legal fictions*, so that the ideals are preserved ... The facts of conquest, high male mortality, and usurpation of land and cattle brought about ... an *asymmetry* in kinship relations such that both the men and the women in the conquering groups were advantageously placed in the business of owning and transmitting cattle, controlling land use, and thus of building up a local following in each community from among the less advantaged and the captive.[33]

Gough's re-analysis of Nuer kinship posits a similar structural effect, a skewing of a formally balanced system, with a consequent marked discrepancy between ideal and reality, such as our own analysis, based on quite other evidence, has postulated to be the case. Moreover, the posited structural imbalance is correlated by Gough, and by ourselves, with the same cause – Nuer conquest of the Dinka.

In the same volume T. O. Beidelman significantly suggests, in a discussion of Nuer priests and prophets, that Nuer 'project all problematical, divisive aspects of their culture on to Dinka'.[34] Our own conclusion, aimed at a more broadly comparative critique of Nuer culture, maintains that the linear flow of historic events is incompatible with the inherently symmetric balance of Nuer consciousness and is therefore projected outside Nuer society on to the world of wild nature. The wild animal is for Nuer the prime symbol of disturbance and change in the social order, just as cattle, and pre-eminently oxen, are the prime symbols of changeless continuity. Here it is significant that the ritual specialist called 'priest of the earth' who acts as arbitrator in blood-feuds between Nuer descent groups, and is able to so act because he stands by birth *outside* the descent-based social system, wears a leopard-skin as his badge of office.[35]

A repressed historical consciousness confronts the Nuer in the alienated form of social relations with wild beasts.

5 Beasts and Strangers

There is a poem by D. H. Lawrence in which the poet records his experience of seeing a wild doe on the sky-line. Contemplating the animal, he becomes aware that he is being observed in his turn:

> ... I looked at her
> And felt her watching;
> I became a strange being ...[1]

Pursuing a parallel metamorphosis we have ventured on the exploration of exotic societies and taken on, in sympathetic imagination, some sense of what it means to live and be a person in these alien cultures. In the analogue of man confronting beast and relating to it we have, while remaining man, taken on beast-hood and now see our former selves as strange, as from the out-side. This indeed, as the present writer sees it, is the whole point of anthropology. Or would be, were it not that in the process of identifying with the other culture, becoming a 'strange being', we also take on a changed identity. The effect of encountering these previously unacknowledged worlds from savannah and forest is a shock of self-awareness, as unexamined assumptions of our own culture emerge suddenly from the comfortable obscurity of unconsciousness and trouble us with the enigmatic outlines of some strange creature. Take as an example the idea of history in modern Western culture. There is a sense of imbalance, in-creasing with the quickening pace of technological change. Existing social forms are constantly menaced with dissolution as new ones struggle for definition and recognition. In the most articulate expressions of this Western sense of history there is a feeling as of the present being overshadowed and dominated by the future. Consider these words by the Hegelian Marxist Georg Lukàcs: 'Man must be able to comprehend the present as a becoming. He can do this by seeing the tendencies out of whose dialectical opposition he can make the future . . . Only he who is willing and whose mission it is to create the future can see the present in its concrete truth.'[2]

This statement expresses a view of the world which is as natural to the Western businessman, alert for novel marketing opportunities, as it is to the communist theoretician. It is also thoroughly culture-bound, as we can see if we consider how small a response it would evoke in Nuer society. There, as we have seen, consciousness is structured by a pervasive balance between opposing tendencies. The dialectic on which Marxism sets such store is arrested and sterilized, discharging itself unproductively in the oscillating process of lineage fission and fusion as determined by the exigencies of the blood feud. No new social forms emerge. We are, however, far from Utopia. As we have also seen, the idyllic stability of the total system is maintained only at the price of a repressed sense of history, which is transformed by the internal logic of Nuer symbolism into the concept of relations between people and wild animals. What is in fact a social relationship of disequilibrium and chronic imbalance, between Nuer and Dinka, assumes the unrecognizable, alienated form of the institution of balanced, reciprocal and ideally enduring relationships between men and beasts of the savannah.

Let us be clear what we are asserting here. Nuer are aware of a long tradition in their society of aggression against the Dinka. But they conceive of this hostile relationship between the two people not as a historical process but as a continuing state or custom, legitimized by myth. In Evans-Pritchard's words, 'raiding of the Dinka is conceived by them to be a normal state of affairs and a duty'.[3] This 'normal state of affairs' is clearly not expected to change or lead to a different social situation. Yet a sense of historical process does exist in the Nuer pysche, although outside conscious awareness. It remains cocooned, as it were, in the polysemic image of twinship between lineage ancestor and wild animal. It cannot therefore be said that Nuer lack a sense of history but rather that they repress it. It continues nevertheless to exist, but outside their consciousness and against it, projected on to the world of wild nature which encompasses their community.

History, the idea of collective social process, is repressed by Nuer consciousness because it is incompatible with the principle of balanced opposition which pervades their cosmos and is conceptually crystallized in the equation of twins and birds. But by the same token the notion of balanced opposition is 'false consciousness' in the Marxist sense, serving as it does to mask the historical process of Nuer domination and absorption of Dinka people and territory. It is relevant to note here that Evans-Pritchard speculatively posits a causal connection between, on the one hand, the 'remarkable size' of Nuer tribes, the relative peace obtaining between them, and their cultural homogeneity, and, on the other hand, the persistent aggression of Nuer against the Dinka.[4]

Lele culture also blocks awareness of collective social process, or history, but in a very different way. Writing of the cross-cutting associations created by the age-set organization in each village community, the Belgian anthropologist Luc de Heusch comments:

> What we have here is a double dualistic structure. The rigid opposition of the two 'hands' expresses a *tension*, radically separating successive generations. But inside each 'hand' the institutionalized collaboration between alternate generations seeks to mask a much more deep-seated socio-economic contradiction. This second dualism cunningly obscures behind an unbalanced system of reciprocal obligations the opposition between the collectivity of elder men (split between the two 'hands') who together control the women, debts in women and material wealth, and the collectivity of younger men (similarly split between the two 'hands').[5]

The truth of the matter is more complex than this interpretation would suggest. The younger men are not deceived by the formal equilibrium of the age-set system; rather, they unconsciously collude with the old men to exclude history from their calculations. But, as de Heusch justly remarks, 'if the structure of the village resides in the age-set system, its uncertain history is bound up with the clans . . . The age-sets belong to a residential structure, localized in space. The clans exist only in time. They are divided higgledy-piggledy in a series of local sections of constantly unstable composition. The village exists in the synchronic dimension (*vit dans la synchronie*), the clan in the temporal dimension (*la diachronie*).'[6]

History is thus relegated to a subsidiary domain of Lele society, that of the clan system. For the village community; which is the main arena of Lele social interaction, history appears only as a disintegrative force. The social game of rights and debts in women is played out in a timeless present, in which rules, rewards and penalties are fixed and unchanging. Only on this understanding can the younger men be expected to give their consent to the privileged position of the elders, knowing it will one day be theirs. As Douglas describes it, the game began to be up for the Lele only after the Second World War. The first obvious sign of crisis for the system was that raffia, the currency in which social prestige is expressed, became increasingly scarce as Lele began to be employed in agriculture and wage labour. The only response Lele could make within the traditional system was to extend credit ever further into the future. The fragile system collapsed when the local missionaries attracted numbers of girl converts who then became available for Christian marriage to the younger men, so breaking the traditional monopoly of the Lele elders over the chief good of their society.[7] The whole structure of the Lele social order then caved in. In ten years the missionaries 'succeeded in smashing the framework of the pagan society, age-sets, polyandry, ordeals and the rest, so well that the ethnographer's task was already one of reconstruction rather than of straight observation'.[8] The missionary-precipitated collapse of Lele society seems to have begun about 1950. By 1953 Lele country was well integrated into the market economy of the Congo with a chain of newly established retail shops doing flourishing business.[9]

The survival of Lele society in its old form had depended on the rigorous exclusion of history, the unpredictable flow of events, from its neatly demarcated world of calculation. Conception and death, events which in many other societies are accepted as fortuitous, were attributed by Lele to the operation of good and evil powers outside their society, and therefore as subject to esoteric law. The social system was underpinned by assigning to the village an inferior and subordinate position in relation to the forest, a dark realm which represented, as we have seen, the hidden communal side of man's nature as opposed to his everyday, individual *persona*. The mystic union and identity of these two aspects of human nature was symbolized in the rite of the pangolin, ultimate and essential oneness being asserted in the fiction by which this animal was supposed to come to the village, there to reign as a king. In its morphology and habits, this strange creature itself stood both for the rigorous discriminations which were the rules of the 'game' of Lele secular society, and for the merging of all differentia in a cosmic unity. Looking back at this disappearing society,[10] it resembles a delicate experiment set up to prove the ultimate identity of the analytic and synthetic modes of human consciousness. The experiment collapsed when the secret of the pangolin became the property of all instead of remaining a formula committed to the charge of a privileged few. Exposed to the light of common day, the treasure dissolved.

Where the Nuer kept awareness of social transformation at a distance, in the marginal territory between the worlds of men and of wild nature, Lele allowed it into their midst, in the enigmatic form of *manis tricuspis*, the pangolin or scaly ant-eater. Where Nuer society keeps its basic contradictions permanently unresolved, as symbolized in the key concept of twinship, Lele society had the temerity to posit a resolution, albeit carefully concealed in the secret lore of a privileged minority cult. And where Nuer society has remained to this day substantially impervious to external influences, whether religious, commercial, political or military, Lele social structure crumbled as soon as the local missionary order made a direct attack on its central value. By committing themselves to an ideal of total integration the Lele made themselves totally vulnerable to external forces.

As we have seen earlier, Lele culture is to be understood as one in which the social centre of gravity is displaced outside the world of human affairs, the village community, on to the non-human world of the forest. The deepest meaning of life for Lele comes from this external realm into the village, even though it is men who have first to go out and actively seek this meaning in the ritual of the communal hunt. Here the primacy of nature over man, forest over village, is to be understood as a symbolic representation of the primacy assigned to the undifferentiated communal aspect of the social relations between members of the same village, as opposed to the relations of individually differentiated men and women engaged in the rational calculation of private advantage. Such a cosmological scheme assigns no place to external *human* intervention in the affairs of the village; it necessarily excludes history, relegating it to the subsidiary domain of the structureless clan, which is to say to limbo. Its fatal weakness is that it presupposes a closed universe, in which there are no surprises.

The universe of the Fipa represents a third option, as it were. Here the social centre of gravity is placed firmly inside the village community. For all Fipa, the village which epitomizes the many scattered settlements of Fipa country is Milansi, 'the eternal village', which has supposedly existed ever since the first man and woman fell to earth there from heaven. But all Fipa villages share in some degree this quality of fixity. By comparison with the settlements of other Central and East African peoples, Fipa villages are remarkably stable in time and space. Most of them have been in existence so long that their present inhabitants do not remember who founded them. Settlements less than twenty-five years old are rare. Nor do villagers migrate *en masse* from time to time in search of fresh land, as do the near-neighbours of the Fipa, the Bemba.[11] Instead, the Fipa village stays put and villagers go out and find the plots they need, if necessary building small huts near by where they can shelter and sleep at periods of intensive agricultural labour. The typical Fipa village is a continuing entity like a state or a modern business corporation. It transcends the lives and personalities of the individuals composing it at any particular time. Individuals and families come and go, but the village goes on.

At first sight this unity and corporate identity of the Fipa village suggests a similarity to the Lele village. But the apparent likeness is deceptive. Where the integration of the Lele village community depends, as we have seen, on the careful separation of component sub-groups within a complex and rigidly bounded structure, the Fipa village community altogether lacks such clear-cut external boundaries and internal subdivisions. At least until we reach the ultimate component unit, the individual person. It is here that Fipa culture does establish clear lines of demarcation, while Lele culture seeks to minimize individual distinctiveness in favour of the cohesion of the sub-group. A man's loyalty to his age-mates is a paramount Lele value:

Age-mates should have no secrets or reserves. They should share their goods and bear one another's hardships. No sacrifice was too great for an age-mate. In a fable, the eagle and the tortoise made a pact of friendship (*ku wat bumbai*: to tie the bond of age-mates). Each promised to the other the most precious thing he possessed. The tortoise asked the eagle for his feathers, which the eagle forthwith plucked out for him. Then the eagle asked the tortoise for his shell, and the tortoise gave it to him. The eagle's feathers eventually grew again, but the tortoise had not hesitated to sacrifice his life.[12]

Fipa draw the line at such total commitment. When, in anticipation of marriage, a young man builds his own hut and, for the first time, cultivates his own plot, he also labours to furnish his home with the domestic and agricultural utensils necessary for daily life. These goods are his property and no one has the right to appropriate them. Men place a high value on the privacy of their own huts and resent intrusion into them.*

Outside the Fipa domestic unit social interaction in and between villages is loosely structured, especially when compared with the rigid formalization of roles in Lele society. Recruitment to a Lele village is based on the criterion of descent: a young man leaving his natal village goes to another where his matriclan has a local section. His acceptance as a fellow clansman, and so also his acceptance as a villager in the age-set system, depends on his personal compatibility with the members of his clan already established there.[13] A newcomer to a Fipa village faces even more stringent a test, because he must make himself acceptable to the generality of established residents, regardless of kinship. Recruitment to a Fipa village differs from the Lele practice in not being channelled through descent. People without kin links in a village are in principle eligible for membership. It is not even necessary that they belong to any particular ethnic group. Fipa villages, particularly the larger ones, often include representatives of diverse tribal groups, such as Mambwe, Lungu, Nyamwanga, Pimbwe and Nyakyusa.

Yet for all its open recruitment and its lack of internal structuration (no lineage or age-set system), the compact Fipa village has a corporate identity conspicuously lacking in the dispersed settlements typical of most other East African peoples. There is no more than an apparent paradox here. Without a complex and delicately balanced social structure the Fipa village community is not vulnerable to external influences in the same sense as the

* On this notion of 'privacy', see also the following chapter on the Fipa concept of the self, pp. 87–89.

Lele community demonstrably is, or was. On the contrary, it can accept interaction with outsiders, maintaining its identity precisely through social change. In a word, here is a self-confident culture which embraces history rather than repressing it or relegating it to a subsidiary area of social experience. The most potent Fipa myth celebrates the enrichment of society occasioned by the incursion of powerful strangers who yet remain ultimately subject to the chiefship of Milansi, symbol of Fipa continuity and identity.[14]

It is worth sketching the main features of this myth, which so heavily underlines the benefits accruing from fruitful interaction with strangers. The chief of Milansi learns in a dream of the forthcoming advent of some strange women who are seen as coveting his chiefdom. He takes the precaution of warning his wife of the danger and particularly instructs her not to part with the royal stool of Milansi, symbol of the chiefdom. When the women in due course arrive at Milansi the chief is away in the bush on a hunting expedition. The leader of the strange women puts moral pressure on the chief's wife to hand over the royal stool, standing on her status as a distinguished guest, and the wife is eventually forced to comply. The chief returns to find the stranger sitting on his royal stool.

His reaction is to accept the situation and reach an accommodation with the strangers. They and their descendants assume political direction of the whole country, and the chiefdom of Milansi takes on an enhanced ritual status as the ultimate source of authority in a transformed society. The strangers for their part contribute the political know-how needed to set up and administer a centralized, hierarchical state.

The myth describes a kind of primal bargain in which there are recognizable advantages for both contracting parties, and in which accommodation with the stranger is of mutual benefit within a social milieu which has been newly created out of the encounter between the two parties. This inbuilt disposition in Fipa culture to do business with strangers, a disposition legitimized by their most potent myth, is in marked contrast to the attitudes to strangers of both Nuer and Lele. Where the cohesion of Nuer society rests on external aggression, and the integrity of the Lele community presupposed insulation from external influence, Fipa culture has taken a course radically different from both of

73

these. In contrast to the expansionist and predatory Bemba of pre-colonial times,[15] the Fipa were noted for their pacific nature, as evidenced in this passage from the Scottish explorer, Joseph Thomson, who visited Ufipa in 1880: 'They are more of a purely agricultural race than any other tribe I have seen. To the cultivation of their fields they devote themselves entirely. They never engage in war, though they will, of course, defend themselves.'[16]

Production was not, however, an end in itself but a means: after the needs of subsistence had been met it provided the basis for external trade. The Fipa economy in the later nineteenth century was solidly based on the production of grain, cloth and iron tools, supplemented by ivory and slaves. The latter were obtained by commerce rather than war. The missionary Alfred Swann, when in Lungu territory to the south of Ufipa in 1883, records the visit of Fipa canoes loaded with grain, which they bartered for Lungu slaves to be sent to the East African coast.[17] The Fipa cloth industry was well known to the Arab traders of Tabora, 400 miles to the north, in 1858, according to Burton. The same authority records the reputation of the Fipa as being 'ever willing to welcome foreign merchants'.[18] Such were in fact securely established in Ufipa at the time of Thomson's visit – they seem to have been mostly Arabs – and they were still there when the first European missionaries arrived in 1890.[19] One of them reported: 'As soon as one enters Ufipa one recognizes a hard-working people. The least patch of fertile ground is cultivated.'[20]

Pacific, welcoming to strangers, industrious and commerce-minded. These are mutually consistent attributes expressing a unitary world view. The eagerness of Fipa to engage in trading transactions again contrasts with the negative attitude to commerce found among the Nuer, who are described as 'inattentive to the products of other people, for which, indeed, they feel no need and often enough show contempt'.[21] A similar lack of interest in trade held for the Lele, just as long as the society maintained its precarious, insulated integrity. But after the collapse of the social order through external intervention, Douglas reports, 'trading activity went up by leaps and bounds'.[22]

Fipa culture by contrast commits its adherents to an intrinsically commercial and utilitarian ethos. Its characteristics merit extended examination. At the broadest, most inclusive level of cosmology the Fipa universe is structurally distinct from those other African worlds we have studied in some detail, those of the Nuer and Lele. The former is distinguished by the principle of balanced opposition, a basic dichotomy which, among other polarities, sets man against nature in unresolved, and unresolvable, contrarity. The latter subordinates the tightly organized society of men to the dark world of nature, recognizing thus a division in man's self between outer and inner, appearance and reality, which is only rarely and momentarily transcended in the ritual of the pangolin. In the Fipa universe, contrary to the Lele paradigm, human society is accounted superior to wild nature, the repository of non-human forces which it is the business of man to understand and in some measure control.

These non-human forces of nature are symbolized, as we have seen, by the python, the largest and strongest of earth-dwelling creatures. Like the pangolin, it is greeted by the title 'king'. But where the former is, by a convenient fiction, supposed to come to the village, the abode of men, in Ufipa it is men who go out and enter into relations with the python in the bush, its home. The difference corresponds to converse structural biases in these two universes, those of the Lele and Fipa. In the one the opposition between man and nature is resolved by identifying the natural world with the dominantly valued communal aspect of man's self, and confining his individual aspect to the closed arena of the village; in the other, dominant value is embodied in the village settlement and the world of humanity expands outward into the non-human world of nature. The one is built on the premise of a static universe, in which the relation between the component parts – human, animal and the mediating world of spirits – remains unchanged; the other posits a state of constant change as man transforms his environment and, in so doing, changes himself.

Nuer culture recognizes a basic dichotomy between man as individual and as communal being, but does not resolve the conflict between these two human aspects. This cultural attitude, which we have seen to be generalized in the concept of balanced opposition, would seem to correspond on the economic level to the symbiotic relationship of Nuer with their means of life, their cattle. As Evans-Pritchard says, 'the Nuer might be called parasites of the cow, but it might be said with equal force that the cow is a parasite of the Nuer'.[23] Most of such artifacts as the Nuer produce are made from the skin, horns and bones of cattle.[24] Cultivation of millet and maize is a marginal activity, and 'all alike regard horticulture as toil forced on them by poverty of stock, for at heart they are herdsmen, and the only labour in which they delight is care of cattle'.[25] Nuer symbolic thought reflects the symbiotic relationship between men and cattle, the abstract social collectivity, the lineage, being equated with the herd, while the personality of the individual man is represented by his ox.[26] The Nuer universe is permanently and unalterably dualistic and static, with no apparent possibility of dynamic interchange between the balanced opposition present and posited in this system of life and thought. Even the ultimate abstract notion of cosmic unity, *Kwoth*, necessarily invokes for Nuer the multiplicity of created things, *cak*.[27]

In contrast to Nuer dualism Lele posit an integrated universe by assigning dominance to man's communal self, as symbolized in the world of nature. This form of structural imbalance corresponds to an economic system in which production of the material means of life is subordinated to non-economic activities necessitated by the isolation and insecurity of the village societies:

> The Lele system of prolonged bachelorhood, with polygyny in middle life, was central to the tribal economy . . . Through polygyny tradition, seniority and male dominance were maintained to the end. But among the costs were delayed marriage for young men, and intervillage raiding. By meeting the problems of polygyny the way they did, Lele were committed to small-scale political life . . . Raiding gave rise to such insecurity that at some times half the able-bodied males were giving armed escort to the others . . . Such insecurity is obviously inimical to trade.[28]

Apart from military pursuits, mature Lele men spent part of their time clearing forest patches where their wives could plant and cultivate maize and manioc (cassava). They also cultivated palm-wine. But the most prestigious male activity, as we have seen, was the communal hunt, with its primarily religious significance. The norms governing Lele economic activity thus again emphasized human dependence on the forest and its produce (game animals, palm-wine and plants used as 'sacred medicines') at the expense of labour concerned with the transformation of vegetable products (maize seeds, manioc tubers and groundnuts); these latter duties were relegated to women, the socially inferior sex.[29] Finally the raffia currency, the physical production of which was a male prerogative, served uniquely as an index of social status and inhibited commercial transactions outside the village societies: 'So long as the old men could require cult dues and marriage fees to be paid in kind they held the keys to social advancement within Lele society.'[30]

The pattern of Fipa economy provides a notable contrast with those of both the Nuer and Lele while corresponding well to that structural bias in Fipa values which assigns the world of man dominance and control over the world of nature. Its basis is the cultivation of finger millet (*eleusine corocana*). The generally poor soil of the plateau which forms the larger part of Fipa territory – richer land is found in the adjoining valley of Lake Rukwa and along the shore of Lake Tanganyika – is fertilized by a system of compost mounding. Grass and weeds are hoed up at the end of the wet season, in April, and the sods piled in large, symmetrical mounds with the vegetation inward. The mounds, set out in regular rows, are sown with Lima beans. Six months later the mounds are broken down and the resultant compost sown with millet. According to A. H. Kirby, a former Director of Agriculture in the Tanganyika Government, 'this is an interesting example of the empirical use of green dressings for improving tilth and adding nitrogen, and of the symbiosis of a leguminous plant and its nodule bacteria, also for increasing soil nitrogen'.[31]

This is the first stage of a three-year rotational cycle. The following year smaller mounds are made on the same site and later sown with maize, while a fresh plot of large mounds has been prepared for millet. In the third year the original plot is again sown with maize or beans and then abandoned.

The Fipa use of land exhibits a considerably higher degree of purposive planning than the relatively haphazard methods of the Lele:

Each year new forest was cleared . . . Once the branches were lopped and the smaller trees felled, they were fired as they lay, without being piled into heaps. Nothing more was done to prepare the ground for cultivation. The half-burnt branches strewed the field. Eventually when they had rotted to a condition soft enough to be chopped by women, they would be carried away for firewood. In the meantime you had to pick your way over them as best you could.[32]

The same goes for deployment of labour resources in agriculture. Where the Lele plot is worked by a man and his wife or wives, with the occasional assistance of a son or sister's son, Fipa organize cooperative working parties at times of intensive labour when much work has to be done in a short time, notably harvesting and threshing.

The evidence suggests that in pre-colonial times, as now, Fipa endeavoured to produce more foodstuffs than were required for mere subsistence. Alfred Swann's report, mentioned earlier,* suggests that agricultural production in Ufipa in the later nineteenth century was sufficient to allow for a substantial export trade. Another missionary-explorer, Edward Coode Hore, saw 'vast fields' bearing many different crops during a visit to Fipa country in 1880.[33] Traditional proverbs abound extolling the rewards of hard work and enterprise, such as 'Wealth makes wealth', 'What you produce is up to you', 'What's worth while needs time and effort', 'We are judged by what we produce', 'Time is money' and 'Big talk won't build the village'.

Considerable trading was carried on within Fipa territory. The warmer climate of the Lake Tanganyika shore and the Rukwa valley favoured the cultivation of cotton, and these regions supported a flourishing weaving industry until it was slowly killed by the importation during the colonial period of cheap cotton goods from Asia. David Livingstone, visiting the Lake Tanganyika shore in 1872, observed 'a very great deal' of cotton being cultivated. Cloth made from it was 'the general clothing of all'.[34] This Fipa product was known to the Arab merchants of distant Tabora in 1858.[35] It was made on a loom, described as 'a rough frame so arranged that the alternate threads can be raised or lowered past the rest, and cross threads are then passed through on a long wooden lath. The cloth is open and heavy but strong and much more durable than the cheap calico and cotton prints which are taking its place. The commonest patterns are white with black-striped borders, though checks and black cloths are seen. It is generally made in pieces of about six feet by five, each cloth being sufficient for a dress.'[36]

The plateau in turn supported a vigorous iron-working industry. Its products included spears, arrow-heads, knives,

* See p. 74.

various kinds of hoe, large and small axes, scythes, chisels, wood-files, pincers, tongs, hammer-heads and nails. The Fipa iron industry has been described by a recent authority as 'the strongest in the corridor region' (the 'corridor' is the extensive area between Lakes Tanganyika and Malawi, where much iron-working was carried on in pre-colonial times).[37] The production process consists of three main phases: smelting of the ore-bearing material in charcoal-fired kilns; refining of the crude metal so produced in miniature 'blast furnaces' in which goatskin bellows provide a forced draught; and working of the raw metal in a forge.

Pieces of unworked iron, called *ifyuuma* or *ifisuulo*, functioned as a crude currency during the later nineteenth century. Each *icuuma* was enough to make a medium-sized hoe, and would have weighed about seven ounces. The iron currency met the need for a common measure of exchange value as Fipa internal and external trade expanded during the second half of the nineteenth century. The transformation of material objects into commodities, all in principle interchangeable in terms of a single unit of value, paralleled the social process by which individual members of Fipa villages became detached from ascriptive bonds and interchangeable in principle with any other human being; and both transformations can be correlated with the multiplication and intensification of social interaction in Ufipa in the second half of the century, particularly the growing participation of Fipa in inter-tribal and trans-continental trade.

The people who inhabited this changing world might be expected to have had a conception of themselves, and of what it means to be human, radically different from those obtaining in the static worlds of the Nuer and Lele. Our analysis must therefore be completed with an account, in a comparative context, of the basic structure of the Fipa personality, the Fipa experience of the self.

6 The Self as Process

Anthropology starts out from the premise that concepts of the self, or what psychoanalysis calls the psyche, are social products. It thus implicitly rejects the Freudian notion of the self as an autonomous entity opposed to the cultural milieu in which it exists. Or rather it takes such a concept of the self, as expounded in Freud's *Civilization and its Discontents*, as unconsciously determined in some important respects by the presuppositions of Western culture. Thus, according to Freud, there is an inherent and insoluble conflict between the individual's urge to happiness and the development of closer bonds between individuals in the process of civilization:

> Since civilization obeys an internal erotic impulsion which causes human beings to unite in a closely-knit group, it can only achieve this aim through an ever-increasing reinforcement of the sense of guilt. What began in relation to the father is completed in relation to the group. If civilization is a necessary course of development from the family to humanity as a whole, then – as a result of the inborn conflict arising from ambivalence, of the eternal struggle between the trends of love and death – there is inextricably bound up with it an increase of the sense of guilt, which will perhaps reach heights that the individual finds hard to tolerate.[1]

Here Freud is simply restating in modern, psychoanalytic terms a concept of the human self as antithetical to its social environment which has been a recurrent theme in Western thought since pre-classical Greece.* In other words, while

* For a summary of the evidence on this point, see R. A. Nisbet, *Social Change and History: Aspects of the Western Theory of Development*, 1969. Nisbet's account of Western social theory suggests that the Freudian, and Rousseau-esque, notion of individual degeneration as a concomitant of material and intellectual progress is one of two persistent and alternative rationalizations in Western culture of an underlying premise which is couched

Freud's model of the human psyche may accurately represent the condition of contemporary Western man, it would be premature to accept it as universally valid.

Godfrey Lienhardt, the ethnographer of the Dinka, has emphasized how profoundly Dinka conceptions of the self differ from our Western ideas. 'The Dinka have no conception which at all closely corresponds to our popular modern conception of the "mind" as mediating and, as it were, storing up the experience of the self. There is for them no such interior entity to appear, on reflection, to stand between the experiencing self at any given moment and what is or has been an exterior influence upon the self.'[2]

Dr Lienhardt quotes the case of a Dinka man who had been imprisoned in Khartoum who called one of his children 'Khartoum' in memory of the place, 'but also to turn aside any possible harmful influence of that place upon him in later life'.[3] What Western man would call a 'memory', related to a past experience, Dinka conceive as an exterior agency still potent to act upon them. Where the individual in Western culture encapsulates his personal past within himself, Dinka experience what Western man would regard as interior, psychic phenomena as features of a timeless external world. Both the boundaries of the self and the nature of the external world are differently conceived, and experienced, by Dinka and by Western man.

Though the subject has been as yet inadequately explored, it seems likely that the Dinka concept of the self, far from being typical of 'primitive' societies in general, is one of many possible models for which a taxonomy has yet to be constructed.[4] It would seem to differ in certain basic features from that of the culturally and linguistically cognate Nuer. The full analysis these differences merit is beyond the scope of this book, but the main impression left by Lienhardt's sensitive exegesis of Dinka thought is of an active striving towards integration of the cosmos and the psyche, in contrast with Nuer acceptance of division in all dimensions of experience.

The sacrifice of cattle, particularly oxen, is the cardinal ritual act among both these Nilotic peoples. Yet while the Dinka

---

in a metaphor of biological 'growth' (*physis*). The opposed version, which has an equally long ancestry, sees science and material progress as promoting individual well-being.

sacrifice a god, the Nuer, according to Evans-Pritchard, sacrifice themselves. Dinka sacrifice is a symbolic drama in which the participants 'try to bring together the parts of their world which were once united' and in which a conscious effort is made to harmonize human experience with human ideals:

the main oral rites . . . assert by a combination of assertions of control and admissions of weakness a relationship between freedom and contingency in human life, in which freedom appears eventually as the stronger . . . In victimizing a bull or an ox the Dinka are aware of using or manipulating something physically more powerful than themselves; and through the identification of the victim with the divinities they also control something spiritually more powerful.[5]

Nuer sacrifice has a more limited aim. Its purpose is 'to establish communication with God rather in order to keep him away or get rid of him than to establish a union or fellowship with him'.[6] When a Nuer sacrifices an ox, as Evans-Pritchard has convincingly argued, the animal represents the man, who 'identifies that part of himself which is evil with the victim so that in its death that part may be eliminated and flow away in its blood'.[7]

The climactic moment of Nuer religion, the sacrifice, epitomizes the balanced opposition pervading all dimensions of their universe. Sacrificing man and sacrificial ox are involved in a drama, as Evans-Pritchard observes.[8] Before immolation the man places his right hand on the animal's back, and in so doing symbolically identifies himself with the beast.* In the final act, the ritual slaughter of the ox, the Nuer in a sense has it both ways, for, as Beidelman remarks in his perceptive gloss on Evans-Pritchard's interpretation of Nuer sacrifice, 'the death of an ox is both a symbolic model to Nuer men of the social processes of their society and also a kind of pledge to Spirit that Nuer remain aware of moral order, even though they cannot and do not wish to conform to it entirely in all stages of their everyday lives'.[9]

And, as Evans-Pritchard says, it is the ox that dies in the sacrificial drama, not the man.[10] The symbolic identification of man with ox and ox with man is possible only because the two beings remain at another level, outside the ritual context, distinct

---

* In this rite, called *buk*, the man at the same time rubs cattle-dung ashes from the home fire lightly on the animal's back, in a gesture of consecration.

and opposed. The substitution of ox for man in Nuer sacrifice, their opposition in terms of momentary equality, mirrors the balanced opposition in the Nuer psyche between the ideal and the real, what ought to be and what is, the communal norm embodied in the concept of agnation and the individualism inherent in lineage segmentation.

Lele reject the commonsense solution – or rather lack of solution – of the Nuer to the problem posed by man's division into logically contradictory components. For them man's self is divided, as it is for the Nuer, into communal and individual aspects. But whereas for the Nuer both elements coexist in the everyday life of village and cattle camp, Lele image the division in a topological metaphor, the neatly demarcated village being identified with the explicitly rule-governed world of individual interaction, and the wild forest with the hidden realm of man's communal self, the domain of the heart with its secret laws. The Nuer make no such investment of themselves in external nature: 'Nuer take nature for granted and are passive and resigned towards it . . . What happens there is the will of God, and that has to be accepted.'[11]

With Lele, on the contrary, this part of the universe is not only the locus of part of themselves, but the very ground of their being. Lele thought and behaviour reflects the primacy accorded to this aspect of the divided self, so much so that the overt world of individual competition is reduced to the status of a mere, albeit complex, game. The division in the Lele self is thus not fundamental and permanent, as with the Nuer, but an appearance only. At a deeper level the Lele self, like the Lele universe, is integral. Individuals know the secrets of their own hearts, since custom imposes on them the obligation to divulge negative thoughts and feelings before embarking on the supreme ritual enterprise, the communal hunt. Ritual experts understand the mysterious laws observed by the forest-dwelling spirits, who are the images * of the forces operating in the communal self.

Both Nuer and Lele conceptions of the self provide useful comparisons with the Fipa. We have seen that the Fipa universe is conversely structured to the Lele, in assigning dominance to

* To adapt a useful term employed by Lienhardt (1961, 157 ff.), who speaks of Dinka divinities as 'imaging' this people's collective experience·

the world of village society as against the non-human world of nature. Social interaction in the village community is far from a game: rather is it the core and essence of human life. What structures Fipa consciousness is quite another dichotomy, and it divides the self just as it divides the wider universe: between the known and the unknown.

Here it is important to realize that in both cosmic and psychic dimensions the way in which Fipa present matters to themselves throws the primary emphasis on the process of interaction between the opposed entities, rather than on the fact of duality. We shall need to consider later how much the implicit and explicit assumptions of Fipa culture are a part also of Western culture. Let us note for the moment that, in contrast to the closed universe of the Lele, the Fipa universe is an open one in which the frontiers of the known expand constantly and, in theory, without limit. We have seen that this world view involves Fipa in the acceptance of continual social change. In the field of cognition, Fipa recognize that the process of knowing is similarly unending. 'What is in the spoon, is potent but what is in the pot beats it,'* asserts one proverb. Another, perhaps more poetically, says that 'He makes an inventory of the stars – and dawn breaks before he's even begun!'† Nevertheless Fipa are committed by their basic values to the active endeavour to extend the field of the known, or to incorporate more of the unknown within the compass of the known. Such a world view clearly sets the highest value on the human intellect, creating a dichotomy in which the intellectual faculty, conceived as a central, controlling agency, is opposed to other faculties or forces, in the universe and in the self, which are conceived as opaque or inertly resistant to the intellect. The non-intellectual forces are also represented as being collectively more powerful, having greater mass or weight, or occupying a larger space than the intellect. On its side the intellect has the advantage of being concentrated and organized, whereas the forces arrayed against it are dispersed.

This world view is articulated by Fipa in varying degrees of definition. It finds its most explicit expression in the field of

* '*Caatiimba ukunswa, unnteendo cilusile.*'
† '*Uwaala-intaanda – ing'usiku unga ca!*'

descent. Fipa lack a single principle of descent by which inter-
personal and inter-group relations are ordered, such a principle
as agnation among the Nuer, and matrilineality among the Lele.
This is no great matter because, unlike the case in many African
societies, descent is of small importance in the structuring of
social relations. But relations of descent are conceived by Fipa
as reflecting the opposition of two factors, or forces, which they
speak of as the 'head' (*unntwe*) and the 'loins' (*unnsana*). The
'head' is associated with masculinity, seniority, the paternal side
of the family, and with intellect. The 'loins' are associated with
femininity, youth, the maternal side of the family, and with
sexuality and reproduction. The 'loins' are also associated with
superior weight, force or numbers relative to the 'head', a
contrast expressed in a proverbial saying, 'The loins are heavy,
the head is light.'*

The everyday behaviour of Fipa is strongly influenced by the
attributes which this conceptual opposition invests in male and
female. Fipa men are generally models of urbane self-control,
even in drink, to which they are much given. Women generally
have louder voices, gesticulate more often and more vigorously,
and are prone to fly into sudden rages, and to give vent to
obscene abuse. Probably much of this emotional violence by
Fipa women is simulated; few of either sex appear to take it
seriously. The most dramatic expression of the contrast in conventional conduct between men and women occurs at a funeral,
with the women mourners shrieking, moaning and chanting
inside the hut with the corpse, the men sitting outside, grave and
quiet-voiced, and immobile.

Other dimensions of the Fipa universe reveal structural
polarities which are analogous to the opposition between 'head'
and 'loins', intellect and passion, in the field of descent. The
relation between the aboriginal chiefdom of Milansi and the
Twa chiefdoms closely parallels the conceptual structure of the
'head'–'loins' opposition. Milansi represents seniority and
continuity in Fipa society, but it is territorially and militarily
insignificant. The Twa are junior and derive their political
legitimacy from Milansi, but dispose of vastly superior wealth
and power. The whole of Ufipa remains nevertheless under the

* '*Ukunnsana kwanwama, ukunntwe kwapeepela.*'

85

ritual authority of Milansi, whose chief is also the priest of the dominant python-spirit of the country, Itweelele. Milansi is represented in the extensive oral history of Ufipa as a controlling, pacific influence over the quarrelsome Twa. The parallel with the polar ideas and attributes associated with descent is strengthened by a myth which represents the founders of Twa chiefship as immigrant women.*

The cohesion and vitality of human cultures appears to rest on a kind of cognitive and affective reductionism by which a wide range of disparate concerns are subsumed under a single thematic motif. We have already found that Nuer culture embodies a conceptual and affective dualism of which the Nuer idea of twinship is an indigenous reflection; Lele culture reflects an imbalance, in which a symbolically significant external nature dominates the world of man; with the Fipa this structural imbalance is reversed, with man dominating, or seeking to dominate, a recalcitrant nature.

The *motif* of central controlling force, or intellect, pitted against manifold and partly unknown powers is a recurrent theme in Fipa culture. It remains to complete the analysis by exploring the influence of this key idea on the conformation of the Fipa psyche. Here the main feature is again a dualism, in which a knowing and controlling agency, said to be located in the head, directs operations and seeks to consolidate and extend control over largely unknown forces within the self. Outside the specific context of descent, where the symbolic emphasis is, appropriately, on the genital region (*unnsana*), Fipa identify the seat of non-intellectual forces with the heart (*umweeso*). This area appears to be autonomous, and in principle inaccessible to the intellect. There is even a parallel here to the dichotomous Western model of the psyche as divided between conscious and unconscious components. 'What is in the heart, only the heart knows,'† says a Fipa proverb. This model of the self is in marked contrast to those proposed by both Nuer and Lele psychology. For Nuer, the climactic moment of animal sacrifice is also the occasion when it is obligatory for a man to reveal any grievance he may have in his heart.[12] As for Lele, Douglas tells us that the

---

* See the outline of this myth on p. 73.

† '*Ica umumweeso, cimanyile unnkola umweeso.*'

object of their skilful rhetoric was 'to reach each other's hearts and to coax out of them any lurking grudge or spite that might be there'.[13]

The idea of an area of the psyche which is intrinsically alien to the knowing self is characteristically Fipa. It resembles the notion of privacy, as found in modern Western culture. There is a sense in which what is private is cut off from conscious knowledge and control, dark and obscure. It belongs to a fragmented and hidden world, opposed to what is unitary, open and public. As we see, 'private' is meaningful only when opposed to its contrary, 'public'. Such an opposition is that between the inside and the outside of a Fipa hut. Since the hut, *iŋaanda*, is identified with the Fipa self, something of the latter can be inferred from its properties. Proverbs again provide essential evidence. 'A person likes (or loves) his hut' ('*iŋaanda lya unntu, akasi*') says one. Another states that what happens inside the hut is no business of, and indeed remains unknown to, anyone outside.* A third explicitly equates the hut with the self, in the formula 'A man's head is his house',† – 'head' here standing for the whole person.

A hut has two important, and opposed, aspects. Its interior is associated with women, and with sexuality and death – both pre-eminently feminine attributes according to the way Fipa view the universe. As an analogue of the self the hut interior corresponds to the secret anti-intellectual self of lawless passions. But the hut also has an exterior, public aspect which corresponds to the aspect of the self presented to others in public life, the social *persona*. Fipa attach paramount importance to appearances. The verb *ukufuka*, 'to be good, fine, or gentlemanly', really means to have a graceful, charming manner, knowing how to comport oneself, speaking with an unassuming, pleasing and polished utterance.

The point about such a valuation of the external self is not just its exteriority but that it is a product of artifice. Men, and to a lesser extent women, learn from an early age the art of what Goffman calls 'impression management'.[14] It is therefore appropriate that the Fipa hut, unlike such other self-projections

---

* 'The crest of the hut, it knows' ('*Isingisyo, amanyile*').
† '*Iŋaanda lya moosi, ili apa nntwe.*'

as the Nuer ox or the motor-car of West European and North American man, is the product of its owner's labour. Proverbs emphasize the value assigned to external appearance by the Fipa. 'The greatness of a hen is its feathers' says one, another 'The beauty of a human being is his clothes'.* It is what a person adds to his natural endowment that counts, or, as we should say, what he makes of himself. The Fipa concept of the self assigns predominant value to the active, creative power in the psyche, as opposed to what is conceived as elemental, natural and unchanging.

Clothes, social *personae* and hut exteriors all have as part of their function that of concealing what is inside. The Fipa investment in the creative intellect is such that the individual person cannot be fully aware of the contents of his non-intellectual, secret interior. Unlike Nuer and Lele, Fipa do not exact the public admission of hidden grievances; only active transgressions against one's fellows, such as theft and adultery, might sometimes be confessed in order to avoid ritual sanctions.† Again, unlike the Lele, Fipa do not conceive of rhetoric as a means to 'reach each other's hearts and to coax out of them any lurking grudge or spite that might be there'.[15] Such an ambition could scarcely occur to them. Their verbal skills are ends in themselves rather than means to an esoteric end, and their cultural affinity is with the Enlightenment rather than the Reformation.

The concept of the self as primarily active and purposive commits the Fipa to a radically different kind of psychic dualism from those of the Nuer and Lele. With the Nuer, the contraposition of ideal and real, communal and individual, produces a state of equilibrium in consciousness. With the Lele, the assumption of a reality deeper than the everyday world of village society, in relation to which the latter is but a surface phenomenon, produces a concept of the self as a static and circumscribed field of awareness dependent on laws outside its knowledge and control. With the Fipa, what for the Lele is superficial and contingent, and for the Nuer one side of a complementary

---

* '*Ukulu wa inkhoko, amafuumbu yakwe.*' '*Usifu wa unntu, ifiswaalo fyakwe*'.

† In former times a man suffering from what we would call a bad conscience might assuage it by shouting a public confession in the village, at night, combined with an offering to the spirit Kataai, the only Fipa divinity which was not identified with a particular territory or incarnated in a python.

opposition, becomes the essence of the self. Here, the self is conceived not as a state but as a process, a progressive emergence of consciousness out of the confrontation of intellect with its converse, non-rational force or passion.

This Fipa concept of the self as process has the advantage of resolving the antinomy, encountered among both Nuer and Lele, between individual and communal aspects of human nature. *Ufukusu*, the proper and pleasing display of the self in social intercourse, is no more an act of egotistical aggrandisement than it is of self-transcendence in communal fellowship. Or rather it is both and neither. For here the normal state of the self is transcendent; it exists in the constant interchange of human communication, which is therefore, for Fipa, an end in itself. More, in its widest sense it is *the* end of human life. The exchange of material goods between peoples is a development of the exchange of verbal messages between fellow-villagers. Both kinds of transaction rest on the presumption of mutual gain.

If the self is a process, as it is for Fipa, then speech is its prototypical expression, though by no means its only expression. In speech the self emerges as originator and constructor – of meaning. Which is to say that in the process of verbal communication the human individual achieves self-definition. In the act of giving which is the speech-performance, the giver also receives – of himself. And since verbal communication is conditioned by the requirement of physical proximity between the participants, we can at last understand why Fipa live in concentrated but formally unstructured settlements: it is a necessity of their psychic economy. We have resolved the problem of explanation originally posed in Chapter 3, where it was noted that the organizing principles of Fipa society had 'to be sought elsewhere than in a set of formal rules'.*

It might be objected that the economic necessity postulated here could well be material rather than psychic. Here the Nyamwezi of central Tanzania can serve as a control group to test the theory, living as they do in a similar physical environment to the Fipa and having a similar, millet-based economic system. But unlike the Fipa they live in dispersed homesteads, even though during the nineteenth century they were massed

* See p. 43.

in large villages for security reasons.[16] Hence the concentration typical of Fipa settlements must be explained by some factor other than the Fipa economic system. That factor, we now postulate, is the form in which Fipa apprehend the self and its relation to other selves in society.

In the close-packed huts of the typical Fipa village, spatially interrelated by no overt principle of social organization, and each with its dark and private interior, there is a physical analogue of the Fipa concept of the self and its relation to human society. The counterweight and logical complement to the atomistic individual, dichotomized between controlling intellect and a congeries of dark, non-rational forces, is the entirely public self which exists in cooperative interchange with others. This concept of the self as a duality in which the light, public aspect constantly seeks to extend its organizing power into the realm of the dark and unknown aspect is structurally homologous with the Fipa concept of the universe, in which a collective human rationality endeavours to understand and control the world of wild nature.

The social counterpart to the Fipa notion of the self as process is their sense of their society as one developing in time. As we might expect, Fipa consciousness of social process finds expression in a large corpus of historical traditions concerning the evolution of their society. Such homology between diverse areas of human experience is what analysis of the Nuer and Lele material has taught us to expect, and is probably a characteristic common to all human cultures.

Take the question of personal names. In all societies such names reflect certain facets of self-identity. Adult Nuer men possess two names which can be taken as representing the basic dualism in the Nuer concept of self: a spear-name, which symbolizes agnatic unity, and an ox-name, taken from his favourite beast. Both names will be shouted by a man beginning his invocation at the sacrifice of an ox.[17]

Lele names reflect matriclan affiliation.[18] The clan system, as we have seen, is a subsidiary principle of Lele social organization and the contingency of clanship can be understood as an appropriate analogy to the contingent, inessential nature we have attributed to the differentiated, individual self in Lele thought. As indices of individual differentiation, Lele personal names appropriately reflect a contingent, auxiliary aspect of their social order.

Fipa often have several names, but the most important are two which have to be announced when a person speaks in a court of law or as a representative of his family in marriage negotiations. These two names reflect the symbolic opposition of 'head' and 'loins', the form assumed in the context of descent of the pervasive polarity in Fipa thought between intellect and passions. There are only four names in use 'on the head side' as against twenty-six names 'on the loin side'. The former name a person takes from his father, the latter from his father's mother. The names in both categories are individually linked with objects of the environment. Wild animals, birds and plants account for seventeen of the twenty-six objects associated with names 'on the loin side'. The list is markedly heterogeneous, and includes a name associated with the human or animal ear, one associated with 'all wild game' and two rarely occurring names associated with 'the human being' (*unntu*). The 'head' names comprise two domestic animals, cow and dog, a semi-domesticated vegetable, the fig-tree, and a general term, *insi*, meaning 'country' or 'earth'. The significant thing is that although neither name has any collective implications – people of the same 'head' and 'loins' names can and do marry, the names entailing no corporate rights or obligations whatever – every Fipa man and woman is aware of possessing two such names, and will readily cite them. They are part of himself, and a direct link with the thematic duality pervading the Fipa universe. The dual system of name inheritance reflects, through the particular symbols of head and loins, the motif of intellect in dynamic opposition to passions; and each name attaches its possessor to a feature of the external world, through its associated object.

The purposive manipulation of objects in the external world is of course a consequence of the way Fipa conceive of the relation between man and nature. In any village there will usually be one or more experts who has a special knowledge of how to draw on the powers inherent in the world of nature for the benefit of human beings. These experts, who are normally men, are called *asiŋaanga*, 'doctors'. They acquire their esoteric skills through long apprenticeship. Their clientele can be divided into two broad categories. There are those who are sick in body or mind, and whose condition is first diagnosed in terms of the entry into the patient's body of a malignant external agency, such as an evil spirit; and there are those who desire to better their situation in some way, such as gaining a wife or lover or making money. In both kinds of case the explicit object of the doctor's treatment is to reinforce the inherent strength or power (*amaaka*) of the patient or client, in the first kind of case to effect the expulsion from the self of the intrusive agency, and in the second kind to enable the self to realize the desired object.

Every doctor spends a good deal of his time scouring the bush for the animal, vegetable and mineral 'medicines' of his practice. These 'medicines' are conceived by the Fipa in terms rather different from those in which Lele think of their 'sacred medicines'. The healing powers of the latter, which can be applied to both the sick person and the 'bad' or 'spoilt' village, flow from the forest-dwelling spirits. For treatment to be successful, the diviner has to have undergone initiation into a cult group and followed certain restrictions; he also imposes restrictions on the patient or the community being treated.[19] Lele ritual therapy is thus a process by which a person or group is brought into contact with a higher state of being. The healing rites dramatize the dependence of the secular village on the spiritual realm identified with the forest, with the diviners in the role of intermediaries between the two worlds.

Fipa use of medicines also dramatizes a particular view of the universe, expressing, in the context of individual needs, man's general ambition to transform the quality of his being through the domination of nature. Unlike Lele practice, there are no ritual restrictions to imply submission to higher powers; on the contrary, the way Fipa conceptualize the operations of doctors emphasizes the primary role of human volition. The 'medicines' themselves fall into two categories: a basic stock which the doctor keeps by him in a specially woven bag called the *intaangala*; and *ad hoc* ingredients which are collected to suit particular patients or clients. The latter are the primary 'medicines' and are always symbolically appropriate to each case. The former, though often also carrying symbolic meanings, are held by the manner of the doctor's use of them as secondary 'medicines' to act as an undifferentiated force; their function is simply to charge with increased power whatever has been 'spelt out' by the doctor's choice of his primary ingredients. Significantly, too, it is the *ntaangala*, the human artifact, and not the natural ingredients, which a doctor addresses when he wishes to concentrate his faculties for a difficult case; and it is to the *ntaangala* that the patient or client, by a fiction convenient for the doctor, makes his offering before treatment begins.

As we saw earlier, symbolic animals *per se* are rare in Ufipa, only the python truly qualifying for this epithet. In conformity with the active role assigned to man's relation to nature in Fipa cosmology, the symbolic ingredients in Fipa magico-medicine are deliberately abstracted from the organic unities of nature and invested with arbitrary significance, like words. Thus a chicken's head is a primary ingredient in 'medicine' intended to produce a heightened state of awareness. The chicken is credited with a more than human degree of alertness because it wakes before anyone, and the head is the part associated with knowing. 'Medicine' made from this ingredient is taken by doctors themselves, and by ironsmiths. In virility 'medicine' an essential ingredient is usually part of the muscular hump on the neck of a ram, the symbolic association here being with masculine aggression. Security in difficult circumstances is facilitated by 'medicine' incorporating hairs from the head of an eland, because this reputedly dangerous beast* is said to allow a certain kind of bird to nest on its head. Parts of traps used to catch otters and hares, both animals with a reputation for guile, provide ingredients in 'medicine' promoting success in hazardous enterprises. These examples, which could be multiplied, typify the structure of Fipa magico-medical thought. Man's knowledge and understanding of external nature provides symbolically efficacious materials; the significance of the magical ingredients does not emerge from qualities thought of as intrinsic in the animals and plants of the environment, but from man's deductive thought about them. So a ram, for example, does not of itself symbolize virility or any other quality. The symbolic meaning of the hump on its neck follows from the observation that this knot of muscle

---

* 'Dangerous' not only because of its formidable horns (the eland is the largest of the antelopes) but also because it is reputed to harbour a spirit which can injure the hunter unless he takes proper precautions. See pp. 48–49 above.

is used by the animal in levelling blows with its horns against its sexual rivals. Such thought-patterns emphasize the active role of man in relation to the world of nature and are consistent with the wider structure of Fipa ideas about the universe and man's place in it.

Men with such special control over the powers of nature as the doctors are presumed to possess arouse ambivalent feelings among ordinary Fipa. Respect for their esoteric knowledge and skills is tempered with apprehension that such capacities may be used for the destruction of their fellows rather than for their benefit. The figure of the apostate doctor – the man who has turned the constructive drive of Fipa culture back against its progenitors and so, in a real sense, against himself – haunts the Fipa imagination. In contrast with this dreadful being the true, beneficent doctors are sometimes called 'doctors of life' (*asiŋaaanga ya uumi*). The heart of the anti-doctor, the *unndoosi*, or sorcerer, is said to be black (its normal colour is white, according to Fipa). He is supposed to be carried upside-down at night by his wife, while working evil in the village. This image of wilful depravity, in which the normal relations of head and body, masculine and feminine, are reversed, is complemented by another in which the sorcerer is credited with the power to assume the external shape of a dangerous wild beast – lion, leopard, hyaena or buffalo – thus identifying himself with the alien forces of nature which it is man's mission, in the Fipa world view, to oppose and subdue. The sorcerer sends the bush creatures, the mole and the wild pigeon, to infiltrate the huts of his victims.

In face of such infamy magico-medical technology provides Fipa with the only defence they have, or can conceive. Doctors do a brisk business in anti-sorcery 'medicine'. The most potent of these are credited with power to deflect the evil forces projected by the sorcerer back on himself, so destroying him. Fipa seem to accept that sorcery, the deliberate perversion of the intellectual dynamic of their culture, is a constant and inevitable hazard of their social life,* a necessary concomitant of the freedom this culture claims for the individual and even imposes on

* Except for the spasmodic outbursts of millenarian fervour associated with anti-sorcery cults, in which young people characteristically take a leading part.

him. An aspect of this mandatory freedom is the premium placed on knowledge. 'The child who asks questions doesn't lose his way'* says the proverb. One consequence of this attitude to knowledge is that nearly every adult male and many women have some acquaintance with magico-medical technology. There are no closed corporations or guilds of doctors or diviners as among many African peoples (the Lele are one example): anyone with sufficient determination and the personal qualities needed to attract a following may become a doctor. And because esoteric knowledge is not the collective property of a closed group but is acquired by individual initiative, there is no theoretical limit to the acquisition of secret lore and power.

At any stage in the process of acquiring control over the forces of nature an adept may be tempted to transfer his allegiance from humanity to the ferocious forces of non-humanity; he may allow the dark powers of his lower self to overwhelm and dominate his intellect in a brutal travesty of the civilized Fipa ideal. The more mature a man is, the greater his knowledge, then the greater the temptation, as Fipa see it, to go over to the other side. In the periodic anti-sorcery cults which, as among the Lele, can be understood as a substitute for the poison ordeals of pre-colonial times, it is invariably the middle-aged and elderly men who find themselves accused. Any culture that insists on individuals committing themselves to one pole of a duality exposes itself to the risk that some will find the forbidden option too attractive to be foregone. Hence the extreme contrast in such cultures between a polished public *persona* and what is presumed to be a savage interior self. The difference between the Lele and Fipa in this respect – and it is a vital difference – is that for Lele the interior savage is one with that exalted by Rousseau whereas for Fipa it appears remarkably akin to the dark enemy of the popular mythology of medieval and twentieth-century Western man.

* '*Umwaana wi toondosya asululow*' *insila.*

7 The Sacred Python: Darkness Transformed

So far we have sought – though always in a comparative perspective – to establish the specific individuality of our three African societies. The next and final step is the conceptual reintegration of these three societies into a larger humanity, while retaining the individual specificity of each. Such a task is the proper end of any one exercise in anthropological analysis, and it is possible only because the anthropologist is doubly privileged: as a fieldworker he has, ideally at least, access to a wider range of data than any one member of the society being studied; in effect he has the opportunity of actualizing in a single intellect, his own, Durkheim's predicated *conscience collective*. He is privileged in a second sense because his intimate acquaintance with more than one culture gives him that sense of objectivity which is the necessary precondition of any intimation of general humanity which is other than ethnocentric.

However, it is just here that the exponent of a genuinely post-colonial anthropology may find himself in a quandary. Lacking the evolutionary framework that invests paradigmatic value in Western industrial society, he is in danger of falling into a monadic relativism in which each society exists *sui generis*, in ontological isolation. How is the dialectic to be restored between the rediscovered humanity of these formerly disvalued peoples and the Western cultural tradition to which anthropology belongs?

The escape from the dilemma between neo-evolutionism and monadic relativism is by way of the same structural logic which, as it emerges from analysis, has established each society's specific individuality. On the evidence of this book part of the value system underlying each society's world view includes a specific attitude to outsiders, to the external social environment. This

96

attitude, as formalized in each society's world view, is the bridge by which the anthropologist can make the intellectual transition to the world outside his object of study and ultimately return to his own culture.

As far as the Nuer are concerned, what historical evidence there is suggests they have had little experience of interaction with non-Nuer, other than the culturally cognate Dinka. An accident of geography has interposed vast stretches of desert and marsh between Nuerland and the outside world, thus for a long period insulating Nuer from contact with any but fellow-pastoralists. According to Evans-Pritchard, the Arab slavers and ivory traders of the nineteenth century had little to do with the Nuer. He says that the Egyptian Government and later the Mahdist Government, which was supposed to be in control of the Sudan from 1821 to the end of the century, in no way administered the Nuer or exercised control over them from the riverside posts they established on the fringes of their country. The Nuer sometimes raided these posts and were sometimes raided from them, but on the whole they pursued their lives in disregard of them.

This disregard continued after the reconquest of the Sudan and the establishment of the new administration. The Nuer were the last important people to be brought under control and the administration of their country cannot be said to have been very effective till 1928, before which year government consisted of occasional patrols which only succeeded in alienating them further. The nature of the country rendered communications difficult and prevented the establishment of posts in Nuerland itself, and the Nuer showed no desire to make contact with those on its periphery.[1]

Again according to Evans-Pritchard, Nuer have 'a deep sense of their superiority to other peoples', and he speaks of them as displaying 'truculence' and 'aloofness' in relations with strangers. Apparently Nuer see little or no advantage to be gained from peaceful relations with other peoples, not even trade. Their preoccupation with cattle 'causes them to be inattentive to the products of other people, for which, indeed, they feel no need and often enough show contempt'.[2]

This account of Nuer foreign relations and conventional attitudes to strangers accords well with the results of the structural analysis of Nuer thought-forms developed in this book, for we can now see that the structure of Nuer thought causes an assimilation of external social contacts to the generalized concept of Spirit (*Kwoth*), which in the Nuer cosmological idiom signifies what is outside and held in a distanced relationship with Nuer society.[3] Evans-Pritchard's description of Nuer social organization and customary behaviour and beliefs makes it apparent that Nuer retain and perpetually rediscover their identity *in opposition to outsiders*, whether these be members of an adjacent lineage or clan segment or a non-Nuer group. Even where, as in the case of relations of some Nuer groups with the Dinka, there has been set in train a process of change in Nuer society, the dominant Nuer thought-structure of balanced duality masks awareness, for Nuer, of what is going on. The change is consciously reflected only in the fantastic image of twinship of lineage ancestor and wild beast.

Nuer brook no impingement of historic events on their lives, quarantining change by locating it outside their consciousness. In contrast Dinka manipulate the same basic set of symbols as the Nuer – cattle, wild animals and the idea of divinity or Spirit – but in an interestingly different manner which reveals, mediated through symbolic ideas, a real awareness by Dinka of meaningful interaction with alien groups.

Though resembling Nuer in their lack of any notion of historical development'[4] the Dinka, according to Lienhardt's persuasive interpretation, consciously attempt to reconcile their sense of human freedom with their experience of contingency in inherited characteristics and in historic events, 'imaging' the former in what Lienhardt calls 'clan divinities' and the latter in communal, 'free divinities'. Both classes of divinity are frequently associated with wild creatures, their 'emblems'; they are also identified with the cattle sacrificed in their names on ritual occasions. This conjunction wrought by Dinka between the worlds of domestic and wild animals, internal and external, represents, again according to Lienhardt, an assertion by Dinka of 'a relationship between freedom and contingency in human life, in which freedom appears eventually as the stronger'.[5]

Such a symbolic conjunction, and such a relationship, would be unthinkable for Nuer, who insist on locating the contingent in the permanently exterior world of wild creatures. Dinka at least show themselves aware of a *problem* posed for their society by the existence outside it of powerful alien groups, even though their experience of interaction with such groups is conceived by them indirectly in the various 'images' of the 'free divinities'. By comparison Nuer refuse to recognize that there *is* any problem.

Like the Nuer, the Lele are relatively isolated by natural barriers, in this case of river and dense forest, from their tribal neighbours. Their ancestors are said to have occupied the present Lele territory between the Kasai and Loange rivers about 250 years ago and, probably because the land is almost devoid of mineral wealth and comparatively unfertile, to have been left in undisturbed possession until the advent of the Belgian colonial administration. The bellicose reputation of the Lele no doubt also served to deter potential intruders.[6]

Unlike the Nuer, Lele were aware of the benefits to be derived from a limited range of commercial exchanges with other peoples, but they seem to have envisaged such relations as narrowly circumscribed and implying no closer contacts. Their attitude towards their trading partners was often one of contemptuous hostility:

Although they exchanged raffia cloth with Nkutu for red camwood and meat, they feared and despised them. They would say that Nkutu neither washed, nor avoided their mothers-in-law, their women were badly dressed, and their cooking execrable. With the Dinga they traded raffia cloth, palm-rib benches and coffins, for fish. Wissman admired the Dinga as the most dexterous navigators on the Kasai, but Lele merely despised them.[7]

Towards the neighbouring Pende and Mbunda the Lele attitude of 'respect' was more positive but equally distant: seemingly the Lele admired these two peoples for their skill in weaving raffia cloth, the basis of the Lele 'currency'. They were also a source of useful iron goods.[8] But the moral isolation of Lele from other peoples was in any case ensured by the form of recruitment to the autarchic village communities. Men were admitted only on the basis of common descent with their kinsmen in an established clan section; and even then newcomers normally had to undergo a long 'probationary' period before they could consider themselves accepted in village society.[9] And matrilineality precluded the incorporation of non-Lele women in the Lele social system.

There was good reason for these institutional defences against the outside world. As we have seen already, external influence represented the gravest danger to the closed universe of the Lele. Unlike the Nuer, whose thought-structure holds the external environment at a safe distance whenever it happens to impinge on Nuer society, the incapsulated Lele cosmos had no means of adapting itself to a determined alien intrusion: hence both the negative initial response of Lele to the economic opportunities offered by Western capitalism and the speedy collapse of their social order once outsiders, the missionaries, had acquired control over its chief good, young Lele women.*

With the Fipa we have the different case of a society which maintains its identity not on condition of isolation from strangers, as with the Lele, or in opposition to them, as with Nuer, but through a process of cooperative interaction with them. As in the cases of Nuer and Lele, the geographical factor has undoubtedly played a part in the formation of the Fipa world view. Contrasting with the relative inaccessibility of Nuer and Lele territories, the plateau between Lakes Tanganyika and Rukwa where Fipa culture developed was for centuries a natural corridor linking the southern Congo and the Zambian plateau with East Africa. Oral traditions suggest that the first iron-using agriculturalists, the founders of the aboriginal Milansi chiefdom, moved into Ufipa from the south-east about two and a half centuries ago – about the same time that the Lele were occupying their present territory.[10] The agriculturalists reportedly found hunter-gatherers living there, and entered into trading relations with them – exchanging iron goods for meat and honey. Other migrants followed: cattle-keepers, probably Tutsi, from the north, who brought with them ideas of political organization derived from the Interlacustrine Bantu states of Uganda and north-west Tanzania, and other agriculturalists from the south and west with a less complex, kinship-based type of social organization. This latter group of migrants had substantial cultural affinities with the founders of the Milansi chiefdom. They belonged to a cultural area embracing Katanga and part

* See p. 69 above.

of the north-eastern plateau of Zambia which Vansina has designated the Bemba region. The main characteristics of this region as far as social organization is concerned are the existence of shallow, 'totemic' lineages among the common people (sometimes based on matrilineality, as among the Bemba, and sometimes on patrilineality, as among the Luba, Lungu and Mambwe), while the main corporate groups are small settlements, usually of less than a hundred people, who are attached to a headman by ties of descent or affinity. These settlements 'are created by ambitious individuals who gather a following of relatives of all sorts around them. The pivot of the village is its headman, and when he dies the village breaks up.'[11] Economically the region, and indeed the whole 'savanna' – the vast grassland belt south of the equatorial forest – is characterized by the practice of shifting cultivation.

> Although there are many variants in detail, the basic techniques are the same: every year a new area is cleared, and the grasses and tree limbs are burned and the ashes used as fertilizer . . . An important consequence of this method of cultivation is that the density of the population must perforce remain low and settlements must move from time to time to follow the fields.[12]

The end-product of the interaction in Ufipa of these various migrant groups was a society with markedly different characteristics from those outlined by Vansina. For one thing, the paucity of trees over most of the Fipa plateau ruled out for the bulk of its inhabitants the fertilization of plots by admixture of wood-ash which, as Vansina notes, is general in the savanna region. The peoples of the Fipa plateau adopted a more intensive method of cultivation through the building of compost mounds. This agricultural technique had the important consequence that it was no longer an ecological necessity for settlements to move periodically as nearby land became exhausted. The Fipa village thus assumed a permanence and a centrality in relation to the economic productive process which is not to be found among most Central and East African peoples. The different status of the Fipa village is reflected in its much larger average size of more than 250 inhabitants – two and a half times the average quoted by Vansina for the relatively impermanent settlements of the savanna region.[13] At the level of social organization the village headmanship changed from a primary, 'pivotal' role to a secondary role as representative of the village community, which now had a permanent status and corporate identity: appropriately, the headmanship became an elective office for which all adult male members of a village community were eligible. Parallel with these developments the lineage disappeared as a social unit and as a basis for personal identity, to be replaced by a formally unstructured, cognatic kinship system and by the typically Fipa idea of the self in relation to structurally identical other selves in society, of which the village community was the supreme embodiment.

These were revolutionary changes in social and cognitive structure. What brought them about? The main factor seems to have been the geographical situation of Ufipa at the confluence of many population movements and of several important trade routes – particularly the route that carried both the wealth of Katanga to the East African coast and coastal caravans to the southern Congo. Out of this historical and social *mélange* there emerged a distinctive kind of consciousness, of which a principal constituent is a sense of individual rather than collective lineage-based identity. With this special valuation of the Ego the culture of Ufipa instils a complementary valuation of the Other, expressed in a marked reluctance to make blanket judgements of foreign ethnic groups, or to judge individuals by the external marks of ethnic identity. 'Young man, don't hurt the black snake – it may produce a black fish,'* a proverb counsels, meaning that one should not condemn a stranger because of his appearance – if approached as a friend he may have something of value to contribute. Such an evaluation of the individual generates quite a different attitude to strangers from that reflected in conventional Lele ideas about certain of their tribal neighbours, or in the way Nuer refer to the Dinka and other peoples. During my field research I never heard Fipa speak disparagingly of other ethnic groups, although I did hear members of immigrant African groups make derogatory comments about the Fipa. The Lungu, southern neighbours of the Fipa, sometimes refer to the latter as 'the brigand people' (*Apoka*), probably a consequence

---

* '*Unndumeendo, utacuum' insoka induku, utamanyile cikulufyaal' ikambaale*'. The 'fish' mentioned here is the edible black mudfish.

of the commercial exploitation of Lungu by Fipa entrepreneurs during the later nineteenth century.* To my knowledge Fipa have no such pejorative epithets about neighbouring tribal groups.

This urbane attitude probably crystallized during the heyday of Fipa prosperity in the later nineteenth century. In 1880 the English missionary-explorer E. C. Hore commented on his reception at a Fipa village on Lake Tanganyika: 'Here in Fipa more than anywhere else the people most wonderfully disguised their surprise on seeing me – one would think white men were as common as black among some whom I knew had never seen one before.'[14]

Elsewhere in the same letter Hore describes the Fipa as 'sociable and pleasant' and 'not at all shy'. Their flourishing agriculture produced 'an abundance and variety of food'. Most of the villages were or had been fortified, but the palisades were not in good repair, and 'it looks as if the necessity for them was past'. When he left Ufipa the boat's crew 'were discontented at leaving the land of plenty'.[15] These peaceable communities belonged to Nkansi, the northern and more powerful of the two Twa states of Ufipa. Its ruler was Nandi Kapufi, 'the little cloud that brings much rain' (i.e. prosperity), who became chief of Nkansi after a period of civil strife that followed the withdrawal from the country in the late 1840s of an occupying force of Ngoni from southern Africa.† With Kapufi's‡ accession there began a period of unparalleled peace and economic advance. The military power of the state was mainly employed to guard the frontiers and protect internal communications, rather than for external aggression. All sources, documentary and oral, insist on the peace and security enjoyed by the inhabitants of Nkansi during Kapufi's long reign of about thirty years. There was, according to the explorer and geographer, Joseph Thomson, 'no more peaceable race in Central Africa' than the Fipa.[16]

Thomson visited the royal capital of Nkansi during the same

* Cf. the reference to Swann on p. 74.

† Oral tradition says the Twa led a fugitive life in caves during the several years of Ngoni occupation. The invaders left the country as a result of disputes about succession which followed the death of their chief, Zwangendaba.

‡ The name 'Kapufi' should properly be spelt *Kapuufi* to represent the long vowel in the second syllable, but as the rendering 'Kapufi' is general in the literature I retain it here to avoid confusion.

year, 1880, as Hore's voyage along the Lake Tanganyika shore. He paints an agreeable picture of his reception in 'the town of the great Kapufi', both by the chief himself and by the women of the royal house, Kapufi's principal wives, mother and sisters, 'the most motherly and pleasant-looking ladies I had seen anywhere in Africa'.[17] '. . . There were no signs of idleness; some were weaving native cloth; some in groups were pounding food; others were cooking, or preparing skins for wearing. Everywhere was merriment and lighthearted laughter . . .'[18]

Thomson found a group of traders from the East African coast living at the capital. He describes them as Arabs, and it would appear that they were held in high honour: the most important of them is said to have acted as prime minister and general adviser to Kapufi.[19] Hore also speaks of Arab and Swahili traders living among the Fipa communities on the Lake shore.[20]

The inevitably impressionistic accounts of these nineteenth-century travellers none the less help to substantiate the account we have already given of Fipa ideas about the relation of human society to the world of nature and about the structure of the self. It would seem most likely that these distinctive and homologous concepts of society and self as dynamic entities achieved their fullest and most explicit expression during the apogee of Fipa economic and political power from about 1860 until about 1890, when the colonial period began.* They were ideas that accorded so well with the utilitarian commercial policy of the Fipa state that they must surely have played a part in that policy's formulation.

It was also a policy well suited to the geographical situation of Ufipa astride the main arteries of communication between East and Central Africa and the southern Congo, but it could hardly have enjoyed the success it did without the enthusiastic participation of the whole people in terms of a common set of values. The reports of early European travellers and missionaries, and the evidence of Fipa oral traditions, all suggest that

---

* It is convenient to date the beginning of the colonial period in this part of Africa from 1 July 1890, when the Anglo-German Agreement dividing East-Central Africa between Britain and Germany was signed in Berlin. An incidental consequence of the agreement was to sever the lines of communication between Katanga and the coast on which much of Ufipa's nineteenth-century prosperity depended.

The Sacred Python: Darkness Transformed

Twa rule in the later nineteenth century reposed on a high degree of popular consensus. There is a notable absence of the kind of ferocious repression reportedly exercised by Kapufi's contemporary, Mutesa I of Buganda. Thomson had the impression (probably mistaken) that capital punishment was unknown in Kapufi's kingdom, yet he reports: 'Kapufi is greatly respected and reverenced. He wields an actual power of government, so that his orders are respected everywhere.'[21]

A missionary report of 1898 describes the subject people of the Rukwa valley as of gentle disposition (*mœurs douces*), 'accustomed to obey the powerful but pacific chiefs of Kapufi's dynasty'.[22]

There was good reason for popular support for the regime. By the late nineteenth century most of the important political posts in Nkansi, apart from the chiefship itself, were open to the mass of the people. Only one of the country's sixteen administrative districts was controlled as of right by a member of the royal family, a Twa; the other fifteen were held by commoners. The army chief and the military governors of the border districts, key men in the power structure, were likewise recruited from the non-royal mass of the population.

Moreover, business considerations were paramount in the state system. Appointment to a lucrative post in the administration could be secured on payment of a substantial sum to the chief. Remaining in office then became a difficult problem in the management of relations with the chief and the royal court on the one hand, and with the people of one's district on the other. An unsuccessful or unpopular administrator was wont to find himself suddenly removed from office because those under him had contributed the necessary finance to substitute someone more to their liking. It is understandable that Fipa culture lays great emphasis on the arts of persuasion.

For most men in late pre-colonial Ufipa it must have seemed that the roads to wealth and to happiness were one and the same. Ability to work hard, knowing how to influence people in the desired direction without seeming to impose one's will ('A pliant rope gets you across the river,' says a proverb *) – these were the necessary attributes. If one had to identify this culture's pre-

---

* '*Itoontela loose, ikutwaala.*'

eminent value, it would be the utilitarian principle of exchange. The Benthamite presumption of unlimited good is the basis of Ufipa's policy of free trade* and unrestricted immigration. The same principle animates the village community, with its emphasis on verbal communication, and the state's promotion of peaceful international commerce. Exchange in every sense *is* the process of development of self and community alike, as these entities are conceived by Fipa.

This process requires the orderly concentration of large numbers of people. It is facilitated by the abandonment of collective identities based on the idiom of genealogy, the lineage concept and the emergence of collective identities based on a concept of a discrete, differentiated self. These social and cognitive prerequisites were both realized in nineteenth century Ufipa, particularly in the economically favoured state of Nkansi. The principal villages must have been of considerable size. Thomson refers to Kapufi's royal village as a 'town', and describes its internal form as 'a perfect labyrinth of inner bomas, or palisaded quarters'.[23] Hore says that Wampembe, a village on the Lake Tanganyika shore, contained 'about 150 good-sized houses'.[24]

Patently we are dealing here with a social phenomenon which is not peculiar to Fipa, that of urbanization. The combination here of population density, ethnic heterogeneity, markets, and division of labour between various productive and administrative functions gives to the principal settlements of nineteenth-century Ufipa the unmistakable lineaments of small-scale cities. The people who built and maintained these centres of commerce belonged to a culture which had a contrary bias to that expressed in the Lele concern with natural and human boundaries, categories and subdivisions; its central preoccupation was with the reduction or transcendence of category distinctions in society and nature through their progressive subordination to human intellect. Their interest was in the measurement, evalua-

---

* Fipa seem to have made no attempt to protect their substantial 'home industry' of cotton-weaving from the importation of cheap Asian cloth which eventually killed it. Thomson reports Kapufi himself as wearing imported cloth ('Amerikani') in 1880 (Thomson, II, 219). This *laisser faire* attitude contrasts with a reported ban on the wearing of cotton imposed by the Lele chief during the early colonial period (personal communication from M. Douglas).

tion and control of what was conceived to be the general process of change in man, society and the universe, rather than in the appreciation of the cosmos as a complex whole, after the static Lele model. The tendency of Fipa thought was to translate human resources into measurable terms of energy, or power. Time was such a basic resource in Fipa estimation, measurable in energy, or wealth, gained or lost through its consumption. This awareness of finitude was not without undertones of anxiety and even tragedy which were not perceptible to observers of the bustling Fipa society of a century ago. 'The very days an old lady employs to knead a goatskin skirt, they wear out the one she's already got,' 'That reed you use to learn the flute, it spoils your mouth,' 'The pot goes on a journey, and returns in fragments,' say the proverbs.* And yet material goods are constantly consumed ('The dress in rags, the gruel finished')† and the remedy for poverty is bending the back (i.e., labour).‡

This concrete idea of time as a commodity does not accord with that frequently reported from primitive societies. Evans-Pritchard says that Nuer do not speak of time 'as though it were something actual, which passes, can be wasted, can be saved, and so forth':

> I do not think that they ever experience the same feeling of fighting against time or of having to co-ordinate activities with an abstract passage of time, because their points of reference are mainly the activities themselves, which are generally of an abstract character.[25]

This well-known characterization of Nuer concepts of time has had a wide influence in anthropological studies. But there seems little evidence for the implicit assumption often encountered that all non-literate societies resemble the Nuer in their apprehension of time. The evidence suggests on the contrary that the Fipa of the later nineteenth century had indeed developed an idea of an abstract passage of time, intrinsically capable of measurement. I was told that in every village in precolonial Ufipa the village headman, and often other senior men as well, kept account of the passage of the months through

---

* '*Amaand' amanyuka, yanyusil' ingu ya unkoleci*'; '*Iteete ya kusaambilila, ikuweengany' unndomo*'; '*Ulweeso upitaa, ulupiluk' ifiinga.*'
† '*Itoompola mweenda, unnduungula utasila.*'
‡ '*Ileembo lya nsaala: ukwiinamisya.*'

a year by means of twelve reeds suspended on a string, the reeds being moved along the string like beads on an abacus. The months were named and so were the days of a seven-day week.

The basic measure of value, as mentioned earlier, was the standard iron hoe, or *icuuma*. The growth of commerce and the levying of tribute by the Twa states of Nkansi and Lyangalile must have accustomed the people to a quantitative habit of thought. The decimal numeration included terms for 'hundred' and 'thousand', suggesting ability to deal in considerable figures.*

Fipa culture at its height combined an intense preoccupation with developmental change with a solidly fixed identity. Our analysis has shown how this antinomy reflected more basic oppositions in the structure of Fipa consciousness: the intimate interrelation of the private individual and his immersion in an intense public life; and the division in the self between the secret world of the passions and the open life of the controlling intellect. We have also seen how for this structural complex the act of exchange is the principal end of individual and communal life – that indeed the opposition which is the foundation of the Lele universe is resolved for Fipa in the primacy accorded to exchange. Further, that for Fipa this notion originates with the prototypical exchange of human speech, an act which is at once a giving and a receiving, in which individual and communal aspects of the self are merged. For Fipa again, the exchange of information and of material goods between villages, tribes and countries is a logical extension of the primal exchange which is the beginning and end of the village community. The effect of exchange in all its forms is to further the mastery of the intellect over the (in principle limitless) resources of nature, in the external world, and in the interior world of the psyche, mastery over the dark domain of the passions.

This cultural configuration is akin to certain others which have arisen in history and in modern times. These are cultures which,

---

* Lele too once dealt in quantities of currency (cowrie shells) of the order of hundreds of thousands (M. Douglas, personal communication). But for Lele rational calculation was an ultimately secondary aspect of life, as we have seen, whereas for Fipa quantification was an aspect of that intellectual control of reality which was central to their cosmology.

like the Fipa, have placed the centre of gravity of the universe firmly within the human community, and have exalted the human intellect in its struggle to understand and control nature. Like the Fipa, such societies have combined a sense of history with social-evolutionary theory. Such civilizations were those of classical Greece, eighteenth-century France, nineteenth-century Britain and twentieth-century U.S.A. All these were or are essentially urban civilizations, and the basic cultural traits they exhibit immediately suggest an affinity between them and the African society we have been considering.

What is crucial for the wider comparative implications of Fipa cosmology is the relation it posits between the exchange process in human speech and in economics. Both kinds of interaction are conceived by Fipa in terms of a model based on verbal communication, which is accordingly the paradigm of all social exchange. This model assumes that the parties concerned derive personal advantage from the exchange of values. 'In communication,' a proverb says, 'one spies and is spied upon.'* The strategy of the skilful entrepreneur thus presupposes that of the good talker. Words and things run in parallel, with verbal communication the exemplary form of social interaction, the most condensed and immediate expression of the developmental life-process in society and self. In relation to its expression in interactive speech, the exchange of things appears as a replica or a mirror-image. It could never be conceived as a negation of verbal communication or as transcendent of it.

But Fipa were soon aware that in the encounter with Western capitalism they were exposed to a value system that was both cognate with their own and, from their point of view, a destructive perversion of it. The imposition of Western colonial rule on the Fipa at the end of the nineteenth century† confronted them with a crisis unique in their history. The attitudes intrinsic in their culture impelled them to incorporate the European strangers, with their novel customs, into Fipa society. But Western capitalism, with its alienation of man from the products

* *'Amalaango yano yali ukuneengula, ayali yali n'ukuneengulwa.'*
† The German colonial authorities formally took possession of the country in 1898, but European commodities and ideas had already been circulating in Ufipa for several years, through the agency of missionaries and traders.

of his labour, directly attacked the central Fipa value, the primacy of the transcendental self.

The intellectualist bias of Fipa cosmology generated a typical solution of this problem: by developing a reasoned critique of the intrusive alien culture the Fipa could hope to control it, and ultimately turn it to their own advantage. The endeavour issued in a collection of thoughts in the form of a myth or legend woven around the words and acts of a prophet called Kaswa.* This story, which resembles the great bulk of oral art in non-literate cultures in being anonymous, begins by introducing the prophet 'sitting among the elders and brothers'. He tells them things they find hard to understand, of terrible forces approaching their country.

> He said: 'There are monstrous inventors† coming,
> 'Bringing war, striking you in unimaginable ways,
> 'Relentlessly.
>
> 'You people, you'll be robbed of your country.
> 'You won't even be able to cough!'
> Such were the words of Kaswa.

The prophet goes on to predict the break-up of families and the eclipse of traditional paternal authority attendant on the migration of young men to distant cities and plantations. To illustrate the process he holds up a clenched fist and opens it to reveal some grasshoppers, which immediately fly away.

> 'Now tell me what they are!'
> 'Just grasshoppers!' they replied.
> And he said: 'The grasshoppers are your children.
> 'And they are flying away, all of them!
> 'You remain here, old and dying,
> 'And to the very end they are not with you.
> 'For a paltry sum of money we are lost.'

Kaswa then prophesies the extinction of the Twa royal dynasty, likening the Twa to maggots which he reveals in his

* The name *Kaswa* comes from a verb meaning ambiguously 'to curse' and 'to bless'. Kaswa was the prophet of disaster whose words were at the same time means through which Fipa strove for mastery of their fate. The myth, including the Fipa text, appears in 'Kaswa: Oral Tradition of a Fipa Prophet', *Africa*, XL, 3, July 1970, 248–56.

† *Ifituumbu*, from a verb meaning 'to burst out suddenly' and 'to invent'. The *ifituumbu* are associated with cannibalism in other Fipa stories.

other hand.* He continues by characterizing in a few words the changed status of the self and society in the coming order. Individuals will be totally isolated one from another, and will appear to themselves and one another as passive objects. Kaswa conveys this transformation in the image of a human body entirely covered by clothing, even the eyes being 'clothed'. Verbal interaction is degraded and money becomes the measure of all things.

> 'Everything will have its price: even grass
> 'And the very earth itself.
> 'Those born in that time will be repellent boors,
> 'Incapable of civilized converse.'

The bearers of this rebarbative way of life are imaged in the myth in a particularly grotesque way, being assimilated in appearance to a major product of their industry, the motor-car – an appropriate image of the reification of humanity under Western capitalism.

> 'They come in rolling objects,
> 'Their eyes (car headlamps) popping out,
> 'While from their anuses (car exhausts)
> 'They shit fire.'

Meanwhile the strangeness of the products of industrialism is softened in the myth by likening them to familiar creatures of the customary environment: the motor-car is 'the tortoise', the railway train 'the millipede'. The myth concludes with the prophet going all round the country and telling the people the names of its natural features – mountains, rivers and trees – as though reminding them of the resources out of which they have constructed their culture. He then seizes all the goatskin carrying-cloths (*impaapo*) which the mothers of Ufipa use to bind their young children to themselves. This is another symbol of the dissolution of ties between the generations which is to be brought

---

* This prophecy has been virtually realized, there being now only a few dozen of the once reputedly numerous Twa group left in Ufipa. This unusual situation is probably related to the absence in Ufipa of a concept of corporate solidarity based on common descent – the 'lineage' idea.

about by the new order. Then he goes to a place significantly called Loss of Mind (*Nkooswa n'Ilaango*).

> Then he said: 'You people, all of you!
> 'I am going with these carrying-cloths of your children!'
> He raised his hands high towards heaven
> And sank into the ground.

The people begin digging to recover their property, but it and the prophet have disappeared. The myth ends with the terse report:

> They found a stone

meaning that the people are left alone after Kaswa is merged with the darkness of earth at the place called 'Loss of Mind', but their situation is already changed: the teachings of Kaswa have intellectualized for Fipa the problem of ideology and order posed for them by the advent of Western politico-economic domination. Taken together with the myth, described earlier, of the accommodation reached by Ntatakwa, the first man, with the strange and powerful women, the myth of Kaswa reinforces the sense of man defining himself in the process of internalizing the external, domesticating the outsider.* The strange is brought within the compass of the known, making an accommodation with the intrusive culture not only possible but, in a sense, obligatory.

The symbol which crystallizes for Fipa the attitude to the unknown exemplified not only in the myth of Kaswa but in the whole bias of Fipa cosmology is the sacred python, the earth-being sacralized by man. This symbol at once embodies the multi-dimensional structure of the Fipa universe and binds the various levels of experience together through the common theme of a unitary process. It represents the inner darkness of the non-intellectual self, the outer darkness of wild nature, and the unknown external social environment, the source of the powerful and valued stranger; and, through the rituals of worship, the sacred python represents the general life-process of interaction between known and unknown. For in its sacralization the python

---

* On the myth of Ntatakwa and the strange women, see p. 73 above.

is domesticated in reality. It is induced by the cult priests to dispose itself on a stool which is an enlarged version of those used by senior members of every Fipa household. It is taught to eat millet porridge, *insima*, the staple food of all Fipa. And its scales are on ritual occasions rubbed with oil, just as the bodies of the bride and groom are anointed with oil during a Fipa wedding ceremony.

In the sacred python, Fipa man symbolically relates to the unknown, changing it in the process, just as, in his experience and intention, he is himself changed.*

---

* When the Roman Catholic missionaries arrived in Ufipa near the end of the nineteenth century they made a practice of shooting the sacred pythons. Their action caused no outcry among the people, since it posed no threat to the presuppositions of Fipa cosmology: clearly, the missionaries with their rifles represented a greater power than that incarnated in the pythons, and they lost no time in accommodating themselves to it. Cf. R. G. Willis, 'Changes in Mystical Concepts and Practices among the Fipa,' *Ethnology*, VII, 2, 1968, 139–57.

8 Conclusion: Animal Being and Human Values

It remains to summarize the results of this inquiry into animal symbolism and to formulate conclusions. Briefly, in the cases of three autonomous and structurally dissimilar African cultures a distinctive attitude to animals has been related to a multi-dimensional view of the world, of which the man–animal relationship is an integral part. Therefore, in returning to the man–animal nexus with the object of formulating significant generalizations, we shall need to reconstruct the separate, distinctive universes out of which the man–animal relationship is fashioned in each case.

Take first the Nuer. The main emphasis in Nuer relations with animals is on duality, or balanced opposition – the same principle of which human twinship is, for Nuer, the most immediate expression. On the grandest scale of cosmic architecture Spirit and creation, sky and earth, are formally opposed; the structure of Nuer society, with its nested hierarchies of opposed and complementary segments, has a mirror image in the postulated structure of the natural order; at home, human society is mirrored again in the symbiotic society of cattle; the bovine order is opposed to the converse domain of wild creatures; within the herd itself, bull confronts ox in opposed and balanced complexes of symbolic associations spanning the whole range of Nuer ecological, social and psychic organization; individuals and groups are juxtaposed to wild animal species; man is paired with ox in a symbolic drama; and human twins are equated with birds, symbolic of the paradox of cosmic unity and division, in a final distillation of an all-pervasive dualistic symmetry.

This ahistorical world of mirrored opposites is akin to one imagined by Borges:

Conclusion: Animal Being and Human Values

Things duplicate themselves in Tlön. They tend at the same time to efface themselves, to lose their detail when people forget them. The classic example is that of a stone threshold which lasted as long as it was visited by a beggar, and faded from sight on his death. Occasionally, a few birds, a horse perhaps, have saved the ruins of an amphitheatre.[1]

Is there any issue from the Nuer labyrinth? Evans-Pritchard, the prime authority, admits himself agnostic as to the ultimate meaning of Nuer experience: it is a matter for the theologian.[2] Beidelman's re-analysis of the Nuer material, couched as it is in the rigid Lévi-Straussian mould of parallel and related sets of binary discriminations, leaves us substantially in the mirrored maze of structuralist formalism; though there is a hint in Beidelman's concluding lines that Nuer may find in death a final release from the dualist straitjacket:

In the spearing of an ox a Nuer expresses a kind of transfiguration, through immolation, of his sexual self and an anticipation of his own transformation, through death, into the agnatic ideal person which his own living domestic, sexual self cannot wholly be and, indeed, cannot wholly accept.[3]

Beidelman's interpretation, illuminating as it is in some respects, fails to do justice to Nuer experience because of its concentration on a subsidiary element of the Nuer symbolic system, the relation between ox and bull. This subsidiary symbolic opposition derives its sense from the inclusive opposition between wild nature and the humanized world of cattle. The former symbolizes all that Nuer conceive as external, accidental and inessential in the life of man. When linked to individuals and groups in the distanced *thek* relationship of mutual respect, the wild animal species becomes the emblem of the contingent event, the (to Nuer) intrinsically senseless happening which inaugurates an outward and superficial distinction of the individual or group concerned. The significance for Nuer of the wild animal in the *thek* relationship is an essentially negative one: it connotes the non-sense of its intrusive appearance and of the coincident event, an anomalous conjunction which is further signalled in the association of both wild animal and event with the notion of *kwoth* (Spirit).* The twin-birth of a human being and a wild animal is the characteristically dualist image by which Nuer represent to themselves and, as it were, 'naturalize' such an anomalous occurrence.

But the negative value placed on the specific wild animal, and more generally on the whole realm of wild nature, both defines and is defined by the value of the contraposed world and species, that of domestic cattle. In opposition to the negative attribution of contingency, externality and specificity, the positively valued cattle represent what is central, general and permanent in human life.

> The Nuer and his herd form a corporate community with solidarity of interests, to serve which the lives of both are adjusted . . . Cattle are not only an object of absorbing interest to Nuer, having great economic utility and social value, but they live in the closest possible association with them. Moreover, irrespective of use, they are in themselves a cultural end, and the mere possession of, and proximity to, them gives a man his heart's desire. On them are concentrated his immediate interests and his farthest ambitions.[4]

In contrast there is a marked lack of interest, either utilitarian or emotional, in the world of wild nature:

> This lack of interest in hunting may be due to the fact that their flocks and herds supply them, through sacrifice, with meat and to the nature of their country which renders hunting difficult, but, whatever the reason, they are not interested, so that any killing of animals outside sacrifice is rare; and we may here say again . . . that the Nuer mind is turned inwards towards his own society of men and cattle.[5]

But within the inclusive category 'cattle' there is a further bi-polar opposition which reproduces, in little, the form of the basic Nuer distinction between domestic and wild animals. In the symbolic opposition of bull and ox, to which Beidelman has

---

* This is one of two polar meanings which the dualistic logic of Nuer symbolism imposes on the concept *kwoth*. Here *kwoth* expresses differentiation and plurality, and such spirits are called 'spirits of the below' (*kuth piny*) by Nuer. In its contrary and complementary meaning *kwoth* expresses undifferentiated unity and transcendence, variously called by Nuer 'God in the sky' and 'spirits of the above' (*kwoth a nhial* and *kuth nhial*) (Evans-Pritchard, 1956, 50, 91).

particularly directed our attention, it is the ox which, surprisingly to a Westerner, is invested with value, to the point of identification with men, at the expense of the bull.

We may ask why the identification is with oxen and not with bulls . . . The commonsense answer is that Nuer castrate all but a very few of their bulls, so that there would not be enough entire animals to go round, and this may be the right explanation. Even if it is not, or is not a sufficient explanation, we must here take it as given that the equation is between man and ox . . . If a beast is entire it is castrated before sacrifice. It is perhaps also necessary to remark that Nuer evaluation of bulls and oxen is not ours. Our representation of an ox, in contrast to a bull, is a docile, inferior, and slightly contemptible beast destined for the slaughter-house. In the Nuer representation a fat ox is a thing of grandeur and beauty. It is oxen which arouse their admiration. Bulls evoke utilitarian interest rather than emotional and aesthetic attention.[6]

Nevertheless the bull has important symbolic associations for Nuer, notably with ambition and divisive self-interest, and with uninhibited sexuality.[7] Evans-Pritchard says that a common explanation of a division in the clan is the fighting of bulls of the ancestors of the divided parts.[8] In contrast the ox represents the moral constraint of sexual inhibition and the unifying concept of agnatic solidarity.[9] In terms of the wider and more inclusive opposition between the bovine world and the domain of wild nature, we can see that the bull is devalued by its resemblance to a wild animal in relation to the thoroughly domesticated ox: the bull therefore represents plurality, division and transience in comparison to the enduring, unitary social associations of the ox. But in the total system of Nuer symbolic representations these are permanent and complementary aspects of the Nuer social order. Situational fission and fusion of clan and lineage segments, the alternation between village and cattle camp, between narrow and wide span of social relations in the ecological cycle: these are permanent and intrinsic features of the Nuer social order. When opposed to the broad category of wild animals, the subsidiary categories 'ox' and 'bull' fuse in the inclusive category of 'cattle', which is itself a subdivision – though the most important – of the category 'domestic animals'.

The concept 'cattle' symbolizes for Nuer the identity and continuity of their society, including the constant factor of segmentary conflict epitomized in the institution of the feud, for, as Nuer put it, cattle cause men 'to quarrel and slay one another'.[10] Within the generic concept 'cattle' the notion of 'herd' has a further and more specific association: it symbolizes the continuity of the basis of social organization, the patrilineal clan and its component lineages.[11] But it is in the concept 'ox' that quintessential symbolic meaning is concentrated, for it is, as Evans-Pritchard says, 'the focal point at which the feelings a Nuer has towards cattle converge and run over into demonstration by word and gesture':[12]

If he is a young man he gets a boy to lead his favourite ox, after which he takes his name, round the camp in the morning and leaps and sings behind it; and often at night he walks among the cattle ringing an ox-bell and singing the praises of his kinsmen, his sweethearts, and his oxen. When his ox comes home in the evening he pets it, rubs ashes on its back, removes ticks from its belly and scrotum, and picks adherent dung from its anus. He tethers it in front of his windscreen so that he can see it if he wakes, for no sight so fills a Nuer with contentment and pride as his oxen. The more he can display the happier he is, and to make them more attractive he decorates their horns with long tassels, which he can admire as they toss their heads and shake them on their return to camp, and their necks with bells, which tinkle in the pastures.[13]

Nevertheless it is not with any concrete animal that the 'identification' of man and ox, as Evans-Pritchard terms it, is effected, but with 'oxness', the idea of ox:

. . . a man normally retains his ox-name and continues to be called by it and also to shout out the name of the ox from which it is derived long after the ox is no more in his possession . . . it is not the ox of initiation itself with which there is 'identification' but ox, the idea of oxen . . . Any ox will therefore serve the purpose, or, indeed, no ox at all – only the memory, or rather the idea, of an ox.[14]

'Ox' now appears as the culmination of a set of contrasted cultural emphases which have their basis in the opposition of wild and domestic animals; among the latter it is cattle which are pre-eminently valued; and among cattle it is the ox which is invested with supreme significance as the most domesticated of all cattle, and all animals. Clearly the ox, or rather the concept 'ox', is paramount among Nuer symbols. Whatever is symbolized by 'ox' is the ultimate Nuer value.

Evidently this supreme value has to do with the individual Nuer man rather than any social group or collectivity. For this value is invoked most powerfully, and the identification of man and ox is stressed with the utmost intensity, in the ritual drama of sacrifice. This is the moment when the Nuer self is most passionately committed. For the spear which is, by convention, brandished during the invocations which precede immolation, is 'a projection of the self and stands for the self'. Its manipulation in sacrificial rites expresses 'the throwing of the whole person into the intention of the sacrifice'.[15]

The question remains as to what is represented by this symbolic ox with which Nuer man's ideal self is so strenuously identified. It is a question which Evans-Pritchard poses to himself at the end of his magisterial work, in more general terms, without finding a conclusive answer:

> When the purely social and cultural features of Nuer religion have been abstracted, what is left which may be said to be that which is expressed in the social and cultural forms we have been considering? It is difficult to give a more adequate answer to this question than to say it is a relationship between man and God which transcends all forms . . . A study of the symbols tells us nothing of the nature of what is symbolized.[16]

The diverse symbols of Nuer cosmology are however interrelated in a structure which has its own logic; given a sufficiently rigorous semantic analysis of the general structure, it is possible to determine the meaning of a particular, undefined symbol by inference from the semantic pattern of the system as a whole. There is no doubt that Nuer symbolic thought has a high degree of precision and systematic unity, based on the interrelation of a hierarchic series of symmetrically opposed concepts. But these symmetrical pairs are also asymmetrically valued; and that the single concept 'ox' represents the ultimate Nuer value is apparent both from Evans-Pritchard's ethnography and from the analysis developed here, which itself reposes on Evans-Pritchard's marvellously detailed account of Nuer life and thought.[17]

The ox draws its meaning from its semantic position as the

'focal point', in Evans-Pritchard's words, of Nuer thought and feeling about cattle, which in turn forms the dominant concept in the wider category of domestic animals. The latter category is defined in opposition to the world of wild animals, a domain which stands for exteriority, contingency, specificity in individual and social groups, and the random non-sense of the intrusive event. Domestic animals, and pre-eminently cattle, stand in contrast for the inmost, essential being, for generality and continuity in human life. With these defining qualities of the general concept 'cattle', it might seem inconsistent that the prime Nuer symbol, the ox, is associated not with the collectivity but with the separate, individual man. But there is no inconsistency: what the ox represents is not the actual but a transcendent individual, the inmost, essential being denuded of all external, specific attributes of time or place. Domestic animals symbolize for Nuer, in the most general sense, transcendence of contingency and specificity. The castration of the bovine male is then a symbolic self-transcendence, a harbinger and pledge of which its eventual ritual death is a redemption.* The ultimate Nuer value, to which all other values are subsidiary, is a state of pure contemplation beyond distinction of subject and object, in which Nuer man becomes that which he calls *kwoth* in the pre-eminently valued sense of unitary, undifferentiated being.

Such an interpretation of Nuer symbolism and values is borne out by what Evans-Pritchard tells us of Nuer lyricism, of the lone herdsman composing poetry while watching his cattle;† of Nuer indifference to physical danger and the risk of death;[18] and of their peculiarly abstract notion of personal immortality. Nuer are not concerned with the survival of individuals in any concrete or specific sense after death, but only with the preservation of a man's social identity through the recollection of his name by the living, as a link in a descent line.

> Nuer do not so much think of the ghosts of their forebears as being those members of their lineage who are in the home of the dead, but rather as names numbered, as it were, in the archives of the lineage . . .

---

* Nuer evidently regard bulls as unsuited for the sacrificial role, in principle, for Evans-Pritchard reports that an entire beast is castrated before sacrifice.

† See pp. 15—17 above.

This is the only form of immortality the Nuer are interested in. They are not interested in the survival of the individual as a ghost, but in the survival of the social personality in the name.[19]

Nuer culture exalts the individual, but in a sense that is the converse of that valuation of the individual which is the dominant value of Western culture. What matters supremely in Western thinking is the development of specific characteristics which are at once uniquely personal and socially prized, the source of 'fame'. '. . . at the close of the thirteenth century Italy began to swarm with personalities; here the spell cast on individuality was completely broken, and a thousand different figures appear, each with its own special face.'[20]

It is no accident that the Italian Renaissance was also the period when the Western world rediscovered its sense of history, as Burckhardt's classic study amply testifies.[21] But this concept of individuality as a process places ultimate value on those factors which for the Nuer are contingent and inessential. Nuer culture, as we have seen, consigns particularity of individuals and groups, together with historic events, to the limbo of nonmeaning. By the same token it attributes supreme importance to the inner transformation of the individual, and this state, in Nuer thinking, can be achieved by anyone at any time. Personal renown in Nuer society belongs only to a peripheral category of people, the long-haired, unkempt prophets.[22] For Nuer, the external attributes that differentiate individuals and groups one from another belong to a dimension of non-meaning which is symbolized by that world external to human and bovine society, the domain of wild nature.

For Lele, on the contrary, the world of wild nature, the dark forest beyond the ordered village, is the very foundation of meaning. Analysis of the structure of Lele thought has shown that the forest, the realm of the wild creatures, is one term of a cosmological metaphor in which the village, representing the life of rational individualism, is opposed in a relation of inferiority to the undifferentiated communal aspect of humanity, identified with the forest. Here is a model of collective integration and fully realized human interdependence which is entirely foreign to the mystical anarchism of the Nuer, with their ultimate value of transcendent individualism.

Human cultures begin to look like machines designed for the

production of social meaning. The complex dualism of Nuer symbology issues in an ultimate end of individual self-transcendence in a state of cosmic unity. The carefully defined category distinction of Lele social and natural worlds project an ultimate design of undifferentiated human communalism.

But the real world of the Lele is a tightly circumscribed and static one. Since it reposes on a delicately balanced structure of rights and obligations in the idiom of the pawnship 'game', it is highly vulnerable to external intervention.[23] The forest domain that represents undifferentiated communality, the hidden but ethically superior aspect of man's being, also represents the unknown, what lies outside normal consciousness. Hence the strict precautions taken in handling and consuming forest products, and the attempt to control the forest domain through the imposition of a classificatory grid homologous with the neatly bounded and subdivided world of village society.

Nuer and Lele both oppose conceptually the wild and the domestic animal, but with an inverse value-loading. For Nuer the wild animal represents non-meaning, the inessential exterior of the self and the social group, in contrast to the prime domestic animal, the ox, which concentrates in its being the significance of the universe, society and, most of all, the true, inner self. For Lele, on the contrary, the wild animal represents the inner, true essence of man, whereas the domestic animal is devoid of symbolic significance. Where the ox is the emblem of a mystical anarchism, in which the individual can attain a cosmic identity, the pangolin heralds a transcendental communism in which the individual merges his separate identity in the collective identity of realized fellowship. The Lele appear to have discovered for themselves a problem which has been willy-nilly imposed on the West by its own technological progress: the contradiction between increasing objective interdependence between men with the growth of occupational specialization, and the concomitant subjective sense of fragmentation and alienation of man from himself and his fellows.

Fipa cosmological thought sidesteps this problem by proposing a model of the universe which is unitary and dynamic rather than dichotomized between statically opposed components such as the Nuer worlds of wild and domestic animals, or the Lele village and forest. For Fipa there is no difference in essence between wild and domestic animals, both of them being subject, though in differing degrees, to the overall process of domestication; the same process, seen as the continuous extension of intellectual control over the mass and force of the natural universe, is at work in society and within the human self. Since human communication, and pre-eminently verbal communication, is the form of this process, individual and community participate in a reciprocal interdependence of interests. Contrary to Lele and Nuer ideas, it is the phenomenal, public *persona* which is primary, while the hidden, lower self participates for Fipa in the nature of the wild bush over which it is man's mission to establish a progressive domination.

The Fipa intuition of the world and human nature as essentially a process has, however, the consequence that the intellectual picture of the universe is always provisional. Hence the Fipa cognitive schema is different in kind from the rigid classificatory map of Lele cosmology. Instead of the maintenance and extension of social distinctions and cognitive categories, we find Fipa constantly seeking to subsume existing discriminations and categories within more inclusive and fundamental concepts. The constant expansion of intellectual apprehension into the opaque areas without human society and within the human individual tends to unify individual and collective experience and transcend differentiating characteristics of human beings and external nature. In the Kaswa myth Fipa achieve intellectual interaction with a world culture, that of the West, through the dissolution of their existing cognitive and social structures. The process has a parallel in Western experience. According to the eminent zoologist and biologist P. B. Medawar:

The factual burden of a science varies inversely with its degree of maturity. As a science advances, particular facts are comprehended within, and therefore in a sense annihilated by, general statements of steadily increasing explanatory power and compass – whereupon the facts need no longer be known explicitly, i.e. spelled out and kept in mind. In all sciences we are being progressively relieved of the burden of singular instances, the tyranny of the particular. We need no longer record the fall of every apple.[24]

Fipa culture likewise seeks to transcend plurality and diversity. Its ultimate value is imaged in the python, the wild creature of the earth whose domestication by man symbolizes the central life-process by which the strange and unknown is brought into the light and order of human understanding. The process is an unending one. The python image represents an immortal antagonist without and within; it also appears as a giver and creator of life, for in the Fipa universe, as in the structurally cognate culture of the West, meaning emerges endlessly from the process of interaction between the known and the unknown, intellect and force, familiar and strange. Which is to say that Fipa culture, like Western culture, unfolds within and embraces history, contrasting with the Nuer repulsion of history to the external domain of unmeaning, and its relegation by Lele to a subsidiary area of social organization, the clan.*

Is Fipa culture, then, simply a social formation which reproduces, albeit in minuscule proportions, the basic features of Western culture? The question can be answered by a comparison of cultural values and their structural determinants, as they have been elicited by the present analysis. For Fipa the essence of personal and social life *is* process, that process of interaction between the organizing intellect and the mass of non-intellectual forces within the person and without the society; towards this end verbal communication is the primary means. For Lele the essence of life and the ground of meaning is that postulated communal reality which is the converse of the differentiated individualism of village society and culture. For Nuer the essence, the ultimate meaning of life is the undifferentiated core of the self of which the phenomenal self, the product of contingency and arbitrary events, is the meaningless husk. Western culture reverses the Nuer value-structure. For Westerners, it is the specific qualities of the individual which constitute

---

* The evidence reviewed here suggests a more complex picture than the rather simplistic distinction proposed by Lévi-Strauss between 'hot' and 'cold' societies. The latter are primitive societies which 'resist desperately any structural modification which could afford history a point of entry into their lives', while 'hot' societies are those in which 'differentiation between castes and between classes are urged unceasingly in order to extract social change and energy from them' (*The Scope of Anthropology*, 1967, 46–7). The evolution of Fipa society generated energy and change while *reducing* social differentiation – rather as change has accelerated in Western societies concomitantly with a lessening of the gulf between bourgeoisie and proletariat.

a configuration which is the ultimate value, the source of meaning, the locus of the human essence. Moreover such a configuration of unique characteristics can be held to inhere equally well in a social grouping, including that typical collectivity of Western culture, the nation.

But it is also the case that this postulated essence necessarily invokes the contrary idea of process, so that essence is seen as emerging from the historical development of the person, group or nation.[25] Hence an apparently unlimited series of dualistic oppositions in Western thinking, such as those between 'body' and 'mind', mentalism and behaviourism, humane studies and natural science, and so on. No branch of Western thought seems free of this division, which appears in Freud as the notion of intrinsic conflict within the person, and between the human individual and society.* Even Sir Peter Medawar, whose forthright description of the Western scientific enterprise was quoted earlier in this chapter, makes it in explicit opposition to a contrary version which he attributes to the 'educated layman'. According to this version 'the increase of specialization is the distinguishing mark of modern scientific growth. Because of it, scientists are becoming progressively less well able to communicate even with each other, let alone with the outside world; and we must look forward to an ever finer fragmentation of knowledge, in which each specialist will live in a tiny world of his own'.[26]

The foregoing represents what for Medawar is merely a 'popular misconception' about science which, in the interests of truth, he thrusts aside. But whatever its objective truth or falsity when applied to science, there is substantial evidence that the picture presented by Medawar's straw opponent accords with the experience of a vast number of people in Western industrial society including, probably, not a few scientists. Their view finds powerful expression in the sociology of Max Weber, for whom the rational organization of human labour which has attained its greatest magnitude and complexity in modern Western society is an ongoing process which leaves increasingly less room for human autonomy and initiative. It is a world in which organizations and things dominate men: '. . . the tre-

---

* As noted earlier, on p. 80.

mendous cosmos of the modern economic order . . . is now bound to the technical and economic conditions of machine production which today determine the lives of all the individuals who are born into this mechanism, not only those directly concerned with economic acquisition, with irresistible force'.[27]

In his famous study, Weber locates the intellectual origin of this social system in the world view of one of the most theoretically extreme sects to emerge from the Protestant Reformation, that of Calvin. The bleak but 'magnificently consistent' doctrine of Calvin resulted for those who accepted it, according to Weber, in 'a feeling of unprecedented inner loneliness of the single individual'.[28] This religion of 'worldly asceticism' impelled men to devote their lives to the single-minded and methodically planned pursuit of economic gain; capital accumulation became, for the Calvinist businessman, a sign of grace. Thus were laid, according to Weber, the ideological foundations of what later became, shedding its transcendental objective, the purely materialist ethic of modern capitalism.

The Protestant Ethic and the Spirit of Capitalism is, of course, part of a monumental *œuvre* in which one who has been called 'the greatest of the sociologists'[29] seeks to establish the specific characteristics of the Western socio-cultural order. Weber's analyses of the structure of Confucian, Hindu, Buddhist and Ancient Judaic world views showed that these various cosmological systems were all, in different ways, inimical to the emergence of an ethic of rational economic conduct; thus Weber founded the negative side of his thesis. *The Protestant Ethic* completed the argument: that only from the extreme isolation of the individual such as Calvinism imposed on its adherents could there be generated, as a logical consequence of the Calvinist world view, an ethic of rational planning for economic gain.

There is no doubt that for Weber the social order characteristic of the West, with its inherent tendency to extend rational organization into every department of life, represents the destiny of humankind.[30] The Fipa case is of particular interest when considering Weber's implicitly linear evolutionary thesis, because here is a society which, remote from Western influence, developed a rationalizing world view and a rigorous work-ethic. What is more, this world view and ethic developed in association with a concept of the individual and his relation to society which is as precisely formulated as that of Calvinism, and related to the social order by ties as logically consistent as those Weber has traced between the Calvinist doctrine and capitalist organization. But the Fipa concept differs from the isolated individual of Calvinism in being a model of the individual which locates his essence in his mutual relations of interdependence with his fellows. The two world views are also structurally distinct. Calvinism partakes of the dualism inherent in Western culture in opposing its ultimate value, the spiritual salvation of the individual, to the individual's social action in the world, which is seen as a means to this ultimate end. This dualism is, however, transformed by historical development into its opposite, in which a dominant rational materialism encroaches into a diminishing area of human 'spiritual' autonomy. In contrast the monistic Fipa world view sees the development of the individual and human society as interdependent aspects of a single life-process; there is thus no possibility of a structural transformation of the Fipa world view towards a domination of human beings by reified abstractions, such as Western man has notoriously suffered.

Instead we see, in the nineteenth century apogee of Fipa culture, peace and industry in association not with a grim-faced Puritanism but with a vivacious and sociable populace. This society was remarkable moreover in that, sandwiched between two expansionist African imperialisms, Bemba and Nyamwezi, it managed to combine the maintenance of territorial security through a strong military force with a consistently non-aggressive foreign policy. Our analysis leads us to suppose that these facts reflect basic values projected by the structure of Fipa cosmology, rather than any innate ethical superiority in Fipa humanity. In a similar way Weber himself participated in the value-system of Western culture in his determined advocacy of individual uniqueness as an ultimate end, a conviction which embraced a firm commitment to German nationalism and *Machtpolitik*.[31]

The whole analysis here has shown how the structure of ideas making up the world view of three African cultures has invested the ultimate value for each culture in particular, symbolic animals: the ox for the Nuer; the pangolin for the Lele; and the python for the Fipa.[32] The intuition of concealed significance in the man–animal relation – the genesis of this inquiry – has, it would seem, been justified. The only question that remains is why animals should be chosen for this supreme symbolic function.

The answer is probably to be found in the common relation which all these primary symbols bear to the value-loaded structures of which they are, as it were, projected distillations. Since the publication of Durkheim and Mauss's *Primitive Classification* in 1903 anthropologists have been aware of a connection between the way different peoples picture the external world and the way they relate to one another. Our analyses suggest that the social function of these cognitive pictures is not so much to explain the world, though that is part of the story, but to extract from it a world-transcendent meaning; hence the end for those concerned is not a purely intellectual comprehension, as Lévi-Strauss has so eloquently sought to persuade us in *La Pensée sauvage* and the massive volumes of the *Mythologiques*, but an involvement of the whole being. The purpose of the cognitive relations of opposition, which we have also encountered in these pages, is not to resolve contradictions but rather to precipitate them. Meaning then emerges as the final product of the tension between opposed aspects of experience, an ultimate awareness beyond a merely rationalist comprehension.

Animals would seem to be specially apt to this ultimate symbolic role because, as self-acting inhabitants of the non-human world they lend themselves to the expression of two primary and polar modes of human thought, the metonymic and the metaphoric. According to the linguists Jakobson and Halle:

> The development of a discourse may take place along two different semantic lines: one topic may lead to another either through their similarity or their contiguity. The metaphoric way would be the most appropriate term for the first case and the metonymic way for the second, since they find their most condensed expression in metaphor and metonymy respectively.[33]

The distinctive peculiarity of animals is that, being at once close to man and strange to him, both akin to him and unalterably not-man, they are able to alternate, as objects of human thought, between the contiguity of the metonymic mode and the distanced, analogical mode of the metaphor. This means that, as symbols, animals have the convenient faculty of representing

Conclusion: Animal Being and Human Values

both existential and normative aspects of human experience, as well as their interrelation; what is beyond society, the ultimate ends of action, and the incorporation of such values in the structure of social perception and relations. At this level of abstraction human diversity and human identity are coterminous; which seems a suitable point for an anthropologist to rest from his labours.

Notes

For full bibliographical details, see List of Principal Sources on page 137.

Introduction

1. BERGER, J., 'Animal World', *New Society*, 25 November 1971, 1043.
2. *Animals in Art and Thought to the End of the Middle Ages* (eds. Evelyn Antal and John Harthan), Routledge & Kegan Paul, 1971.

1 Soulful Ox, Historic Wild Beast

1. EVANS-PRITCHARD, 1956, 89–90.
2. EVANS-PRITCHARD, 1940, 36–7.
3. ibid., 19.
4. ibid., 48.
5. LÉVI-STRAUSS, 1962b, 99.
6. EVANS-PRITCHARD, 1940, 41.
7. ibid., 18.
8. ibid., 46.
9. ibid., 47.
10. EVANS-PRITCHARD, 1956, 66.
11. ibid., 178.
12. ibid., 65.
13. ibid., 67.
14. LITTLEJOHN, 1970.

2 Paradox of the Pangolin

1. DOUGLAS, 1963, 81.
2. DOUGLAS, 1954 (ed. Forde), 2.
3. ibid., 84.
4. ibid., 144.
5. ibid.
6. DOUGLAS, 1957, 84.
7. DOUGLAS, 1966, 166–7.
8. ibid., 114 ff.
9. DOUGLAS, 1957, 49.
10. ibid., 48. She adds: 'Significantly, its zoological name is *anomaluru Beecroftii.*'
11. DOUGLAS, 1954 (ed. Forde), 4.

12. ibid., 5.
13. DOUGLAS, 1957, 48.
14. DOUGLAS, 1954 (ed. Forde), 5.
15. DOUGLAS, 1963, 71.
16. ibid.
17. DOUGLAS, 1957, 10; DOUGLAS, 1954 (ed. Forde), 12.
18. DOUGLAS, 1963, 211.
19. ibid., 213.
20. ibid., 113.
21. DOUGLAS, 1954 (ed. Forde), 6. The significance of the demarcation of the forest as a masculine preserve is underscored by the assignment to women of the barren, unprestigious grassland surrounding the village (ibid.).
22. ibid., 13.
23. ibid., 14. In difficult cases, as here, a diviner from another village may be called in.
24. DOUGLAS, 1963, 221.
25. ibid.
26. Cf. Mary Douglas, 'Techniques of Sorcery Control' in J. Middleton and E. H. Winter (eds.), *Witchcraft and Sorcery in East Africa*, 1963, 123–41.
27. DOUGLAS, 1966, 173.
28. ibid., 169.
29. DOUGLAS, 1957, 51.
30. Cf. Evans-Pritchard, 1956, 177: 'They want God to be near at hand, for his presence aids them, and they want him to be far away, for it is dangerous to them.'
31. 'When they discussed a woman's looks, they spoke lyrically about regular proportions, slinky leopard's movement, a face like the rising sun' (Douglas, 1963, 113).

3 Animal Classification and the Image of the Universe

1. Cf. Douglas, 1955, 388–9. The Lele dog is 'hama', polluting, because of its apparent lack of 'shame', *buhonyi*. The Lele attitude to this animal is ambivalent because of its recognized value in hunting.
2. DOUGLAS, 1955, 389.
3. DOUGLAS, 1957, 48.
4. See Père A. Wyckaert, 'Nos Noirs de l'Ufipa et les premiers hommes', *Archiveo dei Missionari d'Africa* (*White Fathers*), Rome.

4 Twins, Birds and False Consciousness

1. The punishment consequent on breaking a taboo is supposed to come ultimately from God (Evans-Pritchard, 1956, 190).
2. ibid., 10.
3. ibid., 268–9.
4. ibid., 269. Why the fox should have been chosen for the role of trouble-maker in these two myths is not clear. Beidelman (1966) points out that hyaena and durra-bird, blamed for the origin of death, are 'negatively regarded, medial creatures, the former allegedly bisexual and eating human dead, the latter a very destructive creature of the bush which consumes man's grain rather than feed in the wild'. It may well be that the fox has a similar ambiguous status in Nuer animal taxonomy.

131

5. Beidelman, 1966, 465.
6. EVANS-PRITCHARD, 1956, 130–31.
7. ibid., 132.
8. LÉVI-STRAUSS, 1962, 82.
9. EVANS-PRITCHARD, 1956, 131.
10. ibid., 129. This is only half the reason. Twins are buried in a special way, on a platform inside the grave, so that their souls can more easily reach the sky (ibid., 130).
11. BEIDELMAN, 1966, 459.
12. EVANS-PRITCHARD, 1956, 271, 279–82.
13. EVANS-PRITCHARD, 1940, 148.
14. EVANS-PRITCHARD, 1956, 65.
15. ibid., 3.
16. ibid., 4.
17. ibid., 177.
18. EVANS-PRITCHARD, 1940, 182.
19. ibid., 183.
20. EVANS-PRITCHARD, 1956, 3.
21. EVANS-PRITCHARD, 1940, 63.
22. ibid., 119.
23. ibid., 126–7.
24. ibid., 92.
25. SAHLINS, MARSHALL D., 'The Segmentary Lineage: an Organization of Predatory Expansion', *American Anthropologist*, 63, 2, 1961, 332–45. Evans-Pritchard gives the total Nuer population as about 200,000 (1940,3), whereas the Dinka are said to number 900,000 in all (Lienhardt, 1961, 1).
26. EVANS-PRITCHARD, 1940, 126.
27. ibid., 125.
28. ibid.
29. ibid.
30. ibid.
31. EVANS-PRITCHARD, 1956, 92. [My emphasis.]
32. 'Nuer Kinship: a Re-examination', in *The Translation of Culture: Essays to E. E. Evans-Pritchard*, ed. T. O. Beidelman, Tavistock Publications, 1971.
33. ibid., 116. [My emphasis.]
34. ibid., 390.
35. This ritual specialist is commonly referred to in the literature as a 'leopard-skin priest', but Evans-Pritchard makes it clear that his usual title among the Nuer is 'priest of the earth' (1956, 291). Beidelman (ibid., 149, note 14) suggests that the dappled marking of the leopard-skin has the special meaning in Nuer, and Dinka, cultures of 'medial, ambiguous status'.

5 Beasts and Strangers

1. From 'A Doe at Evening' in *The Complete Poems of D. H. Lawrence*, collected and edited by Vivian de Sola Pinto and Warren Roberts, Heinemann, 1964.
2. LUKÀCS, 1971, 204.
3. EVANS-PRITCHARD, 1940, 125.

4. ibid., 132.
5. DE HEUSCH, 'Structure et praxis sociales chez les Lele', *L'Homme*, 4, 1964, 90.
6. ibid., 91, 97.
7. DOUGLAS, 1963, 60 and 264 ff.
8. ibid., 265.
9. ibid., 263.
10. At the end of her monograph, Professor Douglas speculates that with Congolese independence the Lele may have ended by restoring the old social system, and comments: 'Only new field-work can settle the question' (ibid., 270).
11. Cf. A. Richards, *Land, Labour and Diet in Northern Rhodesia*, 1939, 110. One of the chief characteristics of the Bemba village, according to Richards, is its 'lack of permanence'.
12. DOUGLAS, 1963, 74.
13. ibid., 97.
14. Cf. Willis, 1964 and 1967.
15. 'Gouldsbury and Sheane record that the Bemba of their day used to brag that they did not know how to hoe, for their only trade was war' (Richards, op. cit., 401).
16. THOMSON, 1881, I, 221.
17. SWANN, 1910, 98.
18. BURTON, 1859, 381.
19. Cf. Mgr Dupont, 'Souvenirs du Tanganika', *Les Missions Catholiques*, 1903.
20. VAN OOST, A., 'Un Voyage au Rukwa', *Chronique Trimestrielle de la Société des Missionnaires d'Afrique (Pères Blancs)*, No. 64, October 1894.
21. EVANS-PRITCHARD, 1940, 88.
22. DOUGLAS, 1963, 263.
23. EVANS-PRITCHARD, 1940, 36.
24. ibid., 29-30.
25. ibid., 16. Evans-Pritchard thinks that Nuer probably cultivated less grain before the rinderpest epidemics of the present century decimated their herds (ibid., 19).
26. See Evans-Pritchard, 1956, 257-60. The elaborated opposition also present in Nuer thought between man as ox and man as bull has been discussed earlier. It reflects the same principle of balanced opposition.
27. ibid., 4-6.
28. DOUGLAS, 1963, 50
29. ibid., 29 ff.
30. ibid., 263.
31. Official Memorandum dated 14 March 1927, and included in the Sumbawanga (Ufipa) District Book.
32. DOUGLAS, 1963, 29.
33. 'Voyage to the South End of Lake Tanganyika, 1880.' (Unpublished letter in the archives of the Congregational Council for World Mission, London.)
34. WALLER, H. (ed.), *The Last Journals of David Livingstone*, 1874, II, 240.
35. BURTON, op. cit.
36. BOILEAU, F. F. R. and WALLACE, L. A., 'The Nyasa-Tanganyika Plateau', *Geographical Journal*, XIII, June 1899, 577-622.

133

37. ST JOHN, CHRISTOPHER, in R. Gray and D. Birmingham (eds.), *Pre-colonial African Trade*, 1970. This writer mistakenly implies that the Fipa iron industry died out during the colonial period. To my knowledge at least one smith was still in active production in 1964, and I heard of others.

6 The Self as Process

1. FREUD, S., *Civilisation and its Discontents*, 1969 edn, trans. Joan Rivière, 70.
2. LIENHARDT, 1961, 149.
3. ibid.
4. West Africa seems to be particularly prolific in theories of divided and multiple selves. See M. Fortes, *Oedipus and Job in West African Religion*, 1959; Robin Horton, 'Destiny and the Unconscious in West Africa', *Africa*, XXXI, April 1961, 2, 110–16; and Marcel Griaule and Germaine Dieterlen, 'The Dogon', in *African Worlds*, ed. Daryll Forde, 1954.
5. LIENHARDT, 1961, 37, 251.
6. EVANS-PRITCHARD, 1956, 275.
7. ibid., 281.
8. ibid., 280.
9. BEIDELMAN, op. cit., 465.
10. EVANS-PRITCHARD, 1956, 280.
11. ibid., 200.
12. ibid., 209.
13. DOUGLAS, 1963, 70–71.
14. GOFFMAN, *The Presentation of the Self in Everyday Life*, 1959, 208 ff.
15. DOUGLAS, 1963, 70–71.
16. Cf. R. G. Abrahams, *The Political Organization of Unyamwezi*, 1967, 12–18.
17. EVANS-PRITCHARD, 1956, 148.
18. DOUGLAS, M., personal communication.
19. DOUGLAS, 1954 (ed. Forde) 7–9.

7 The Sacred Python: Darkness Transformed

1. EVANS-PRITCHARD, 1940, 133–4.
2. ibid., 88.
3. Cf. Evans-Pritchard, 1956, 115–22 and 315–22.
4. LIENHARDT, 1961, 2.
5. ibid., 251.
6. Cf. Douglas, 1963, 9, 187–8. It was not apparently until the 1930s, with the construction of a road system through Lele territory and enforced resettlement, that Lele became really aware of the European presence (ibid., 259–60).
7. ibid., 13–14.
8. ibid.
9. ibid., 96–7.
10. It is possible that the two migrations originated in the same cause – upheavals associated with the expansion of Lunda state power during the seventeenth century. (See J. Vansina, *Kingdoms of the Savana*, 1966, 70–97.)

11. Cf. Vansina, op. cit., 24–8.
12. ibid., 20–21.
13. VANSINA, loc. cit. The figure for Fipa village size is based on statistics drawn from 110 existing settlements.
14. HORE, E. C., 'Voyage to the South End of Lake Tanganyika, 1880.'
15. ibid.
16. THOMSON, 1881, I, 201.
17. ibid., II, 221.
18. ibid.
19. ibid., 218.
20. HORE, op. cit.
21. THOMSON, 1881, II, 222–3.
22. *Chronique trimestrielle de la Société des Missionnaires d'Afrique (Pères Blancs)*, 82, April 1899.
23. THOMSON, op. cit., 218.
24. HORE, op. cit.
25. EVANS-PRITCHARD, 1940, 103.

8 Conclusion: Animal Being and Human Values

1. BORGES, JORGE LUIS, *Tlön, Uqbar, Orbis Tertius*. London, 1965.
2. Cf. Evans-Pritchard, 1956, 322. Interestingly, Evans-Pritchard's colleague and disciple Godfrey Lienhardt has shown more boldness than his master in his comparable discussion of the meaning of Dinka symbolic thought and behaviour (see pp. 81–2 above).
3. BEIDELMAN, 1966, 465.
4. EVANS-PRITCHARD, 1940, 40.
5. EVANS-PRITCHARD, 1956, 267.
6. ibid., 254.
7. BEIDELMAN, 1966, 462–4.
8. EVANS-PRITCHARD, 1956, 258.
9. BEIDELMAN, ibid.
10. Cf. Evans-Pritchard, 1956, 269. It is worth noting that when Nuer speak of 'society' and 'men' they refer always to 'Nuer society' and 'Nuer men'. 'Nuer do not regard other people as "men", whatever their age. They think of *wut*, manhood, as something specifically Nuer' (ibid., 255, note 1).
11. ibid., 258.
12. ibid., 254.
13. EVANS-PRITCHARD, 1940, 37.
14. ibid., 253–4.
15. ibid., 239. Beidelman suggests that the Nuer spear can further be seen as 'a kind of symbolic, socialized penis in which certain dangerous, medial aspects of masculine sexuality are expressed within ideal, moral limits' (op. cit., 458). What is symbolically committed in Nuer sacrifice is the ideal, transcendent self divested of divisive or contradictory elements.
16. ibid., 321.
17. Here I would wholeheartedly concur with Beidelman's estimate of Evans-Pritchard as 'the most distinguished anthropologist alive today' (Beidelman, op. cit., 465, note 1). We are indeed standing, or perhaps sitting, on the shoulders of a giant.

18. 'As Nuer are very prone to fighting, people are frequently killed ... A Nuer will at once fight if he feels that he has been insulted' (Evans-Pritchard, 1940, 151). Evans-Pritchard also refers to the long-standing reputation of the Nuer for bravery and chivalry in war (ibid., 126).

19. ibid., 162–3.

20. BURCKHARDT, J. *The Civilization of the Renaissance in Italy*, 1960, 122.

21. ibid., 145–210.

22. Cf. Evans-Pritchard, 1956, 307. According to Evans-Pritchard, the out-ward deference shown by Nuer to their leading prophets was 'tinged with resentment and hostility' (ibid.).

23. As indeed was proved by events in the early 1950s (see Douglas, 1963, pp. 259–71, and p. 69 above).

24. MEDAWAR, P. B., *The Art of the Soluble*, London, 1969, 128.

25. Professor Louis Dumont has done less than justice to the complexity and versatility of the Western concept of 'individual' in stating that in Western society 'our two cardinal ideals are called equality and liberty. They assume as their common principle, and as a valorized representation, the idea of the human *individual*: humanity is made up of men, and each man is conceived as presenting, in spite of, and over and above his particularity, the essence of humanity' (*Homo Hierarchicus*, 1966, 4). The referent of the concept 'individual' is a *structure*, not a monolithic substance. Hence not only can the 'individual' be a person or a collectivity, such as a commercial corporation, but it can also undergo historical transformation without losing its identity as an 'individual'.

26. MEDAWAR, op. cit., 127.

27. WEBER, M., *The Protestant Ethic and the Spirit of Capitalism* (trans. Talcott Parsons), 1930, 181.

28. ibid., 104.

29. The words of Raymond Aron: 'To me, Max Weber is the greatest of the sociologists; I would even say that he is *the* sociologist' (*Main Currents in Sociological Thought*, 2, 1967, 250).

30. Cf. Aron, op. cit., 255: 'This process is man's destiny, against which it is useless to rebel and which no regime can avoid.'

31. Cf. Aron, *passim*.

32. In the highly differentiated societies of the industrial world such focally symbolic beasts are, it would seem, no longer to be found. Certain correlations can however be traced between Western, or at least English, animal classification and world view, as in E. R. Leach's interesting 'Animal Categories and Verbal Abuse', in E. H. Lenneberg (ed.), *New Directions in the Study of Language*, 1964.

33. JAKOBSON, ROMAN, and HALLE, MORRIS, *Fundamentals of Language*, 1956, 76.

List of Principal Sources

BEIDELMAN, T. O. 1966. 'The Ox and Nuer Sacrifice: some Freudian hypotheses about Nuer symbolism.' *Man*, 1, 4, 453–67.

BURTON, R. F. 1859. 'The Lake Regions of Central Equatorial Africa.' *Journal of the Royal Geographical Society*, 29, 1–454.

DURKHEIM, EMILE. 1964. *The Division of Labor in Society*, trans. G. Simpson. New York: The Free Press.

DOUGLAS, MARY. 1954. 'The Lele of the Kasai.' In *African Worlds* ed. Daryll Forde. London: Oxford University Press, 1–26.

— 1955. 'Social and Religious Symbolism of the Lele of the Kasai.' *Zaïre*, IX, 4, 385–402.

— 1957. 'Animals in Lele Religious Symbolism.' *Africa*, XXVII, 1, 46–58.

— 1963. *The Lele of the Kasai*. London: Oxford University Press.

— 1966. *Purity and Danger*. London: Routledge and Kegan Paul.

EVANS-PRITCHARD, E. E. 1940. *The Nuer: a description of the modes of livelihood and political institutions of a Nilotic people*. Oxford: Clarendon Press.

— 1956. *Nuer Religion*. Oxford: Clarendon Press.

FREUD, SIGMUND. 1963. *Civilization and its Discontents*, trans. J. Rivière. London: The Hogarth Press.

LÉVI-STRAUSS, C. 1962a. *La Pensée sauvage*. Paris: Plon.

— 1962b. *Totemism*, trans. R. Needham. London: Merlin Press.

— 1964. *Mythologiques: Le Cru et le cuit*. Paris: Plon.

LIENHARDT, GODFREY. 1961. *Divinity and Experience: the religion of the Dinka*. Oxford: Clarendon Press.

LITTLEJOHN, JAMES. 1970. 'Twins, Birds, etc.' *Bijdragen*, 126, 1, 91–114.

LUKÀCS, GEORG. 1971. *History and Class Consciousness: studies in Marxist dialectics*, trans. R. Livingstone. London: Merlin Press.

SWANN, A. J. 1910. *Fighting the Slave-Hunters in Central Africa*. London: Cass.

THOMSON, J. 1881. *To the Central African Lakes and Back*. London: Cass.

WEBER, MAX. 1930. *The Protestant Ethic and the Spirit of Capitalism*, trans. Talcott Parsons. London: Unwin University Books.

WILLIS, R. G. 1964. 'Traditional History and Social Structure in Ufipa.' *Africa*, XXXIV, 4, 340–52.

— 1967. 'The Head and the Loins: Lévi-Strauss and Beyond.' *Man*, 2, 4, 519–34.

— n.d. Field Notes, Ufipa, 1962–4 and 1966.

Index

Index

Index